Hinduism, one is tempted to say, can be anything to anyone. Hindus themselves are fond of describing Hinduism as a way of life rather than as a religion.

No one has any idea whether Hinduism accepts converts to its religion. Hare Krishnas, the most visible sign of Hinduism's spread to the West, emphatically declare that they do not view themselves as Hindus. The word "Hindu" itself is not of Indian origin, and Hindus did not describe themselves as such until the 18th century. Yet, Hinduism's adherents characterize it as the world's oldest faith.

In the West, Hinduism is comparatively invisible. Some people view it as synonymous with yoga, which has been reduced to aerobic-like exercises and meditational practices. From the Sanskrit "yuj", which means "to yoke", yoga is a school of Indian philosophy which aims to help the practitioner to come closer to the divine. All this has been largely forgotten.

To others, Hinduism is some vague, undefined and colourful religion with numerous deities.

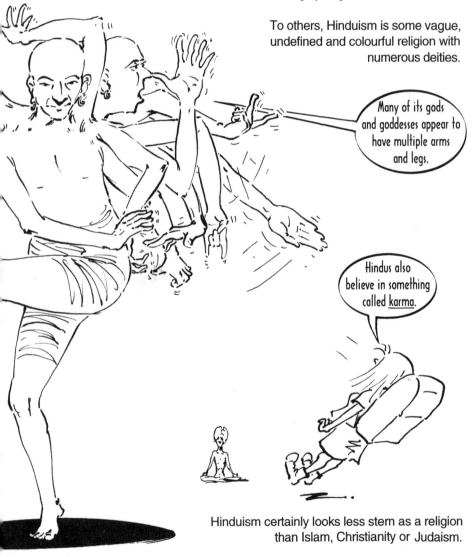

Many of its gods and goddesses appear to have multiple arms and legs.

Hindus also believe in something called karma.

Hinduism certainly looks less stern as a religion than Islam, Christianity or Judaism.

4

The central tenets of Hinduism are not easily described.

All one can say of Hinduism's origins, by contrast, is that it originated in the Indian subcontinent and that the religion has largely been confined to that part of the world.

The earliest civilization in India has been given the name of "Indus Valley" or "Harappan" after one of its most well-developed cities, Harappa, now in Pakistan.

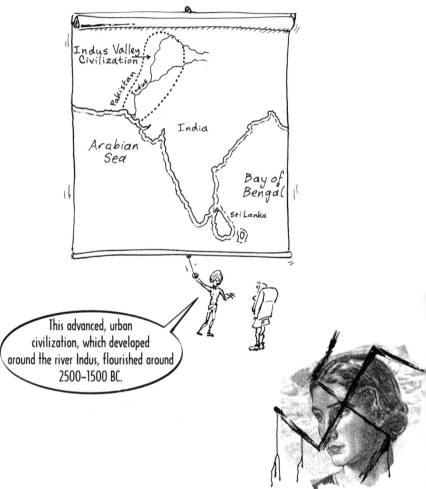

This advanced, urban civilization, which developed around the river Indus, flourished around 2500–1500 BC.

The Indus Valley people, who may be the forerunners of the Dravidian population of South India, appear to have been gradually pushed down south by the Aryans, who commenced their migrations from the Caucasus Mountains (in the present-day region of Georgia in the former Soviet Union) to India around 2000 BC.

The word "Aryan" originally meant "noble". Nazism has given the word racial connotations in the 20th century. The early Aryans were a nomadic people. They brought to India the horse and the chariot, as well as the sacrificial altar.

The oldest literature attributed to the Aryans, known as the Vedas, furnishes a relatively clear picture of their Gods, associated largely with different aspects of nature. Chief among them were Indra, the god of rain and thunder; Surya, the sun god; Varuna, the god of wind; and Agni, the fire god.

Hinduism is generally viewed as having originated with the Aryans, but it is far more accurately described as an amalgam of pre-Aryan and Aryan elements. For instance, image-worship, which predominates in popular Hinduism, finds almost no mention in the Vedas. Shiva, the all-important god besides Vishnu, is almost certainly a non-Aryan god (absent in the Vedas) who eventually made his way into the Hindu pantheon. The innumerable mother goddesses (*devis*) who spangle Hinduism are also non-Aryan.

The Aryans most likely looked down upon the people they conquered as inferior.

Indra is described in the <u>Rig Veda</u>, the most important of the Vedic scriptures, as the vanquisher of a dark-skinned people and destroyer of forts and citadels.

The indigenous people are seen as possibly matriarchal and "softer" in their approach to life. The Aryans are viewed instead as patriarchal and more inclined to prize masculinity.

Though the Indus Valley people were literate, they left behind no literature. The Indus Valley script remains undeciphered down to the present day. The Aryans, on the other hand, were largely illiterate; but they bequeathed to India a prolific literature.

The religious literature of the Aryans consists of a wide variety of texts, all composed in Sanskrit, which means "perfected" or "well-made". Sanskrit is sometimes referred to as a dead language in the manner of Greek or Latin, but this is incorrect in several respects.

More so than Latin, Sanskrit retains an honoured place in Hindu rituals, and is used widely on ceremonial occasions.

9

The word "Vedas" [knowledge] is sometimes used loosely to refer to a mass of early Hindu writings, but strictly speaking there are four Vedas [*catur-veda*]: *Rig*, *Sama*, *Atharva* and *Yajur*. Along with a class of texts known as *Aranyakas* (forest books), *Brahmanas* (ritual manuals) and, most importantly, the Upanishads (philosophical meditations), the Vedas are known as *shruti* (meaning "heard") or divinely revealed texts.

In theory, the Vedas rank far above all other Hindu religious texts, which are collectively known as <u>smriti</u> (meaning "remembered").

The law books (*dharmashastras*), the epic literature of the Hindus, the mythological texts (*Puranas*), and even the *Bhagavad Gita*, the most widely known work of Hindu literature in the West, all number among the *smritis*.

Belief in the infallibility of the Vedas is commonly accepted as one of the three central tenets of Hinduism. Such a view illustrates one of the fundamental difficulties in understanding Hinduism, namely the gap between the "textbook" and the view from the ground.

If the Vedas are infallible for Hindus – as the Quran is infallible for Muslims – one would expect widespread familiarity with these texts.

But scarcely any Hindu knows anything of the Vedas.

The Gita Press, founded in 1923 to popularize the Hindu scriptures, has printed over 300 million copies of *smriti* literature, but they will not publish the Vedas on the grounds that these divinely-revealed texts may not be tampered with by human beings.

Nevertheless, a few lines from the *Rig Veda* (II.62.x), known as the *Gayatri mantra*, have become synonymous with Hinduism for many believers. The Gayatri mantra is the first thing that even little children are taught.

13

No one knows why, from a text as voluminous as the *Rig Veda* with its 1,028 hymns or 10,500 verses, the Gayatri mantra assumed such importance. The *Rig Veda* has many remarkable passages, none more so than its "Hymn to Creation" (*Nasadiya Sukta*, X.129).

God didn't create the universe in six days. Nor were the waters parted, as in the Bible, <u>Genesis</u> 1.

BRAHMA

Rather, the author invokes the mystery of the Creation ...

VISHNU

"Neither nonbeing nor being was as yet,
Neither was airy space nor heavens beyond;
What was enveloped? And where? Sheltered by whom?
And was there water? Bottomless, unfathomed?" [X.129.1]

HINDU SYMBOL OF CREATION

14

There is only the One; but "desire" introduces differentiation, and the wise come to perceive that "in nonbeing lay the bond of being". The hymn's author ends with an affirmation of the uncertainty we have about creation: who can say from where it all arose and what is the universe's origin?

One might think that the Creator, at least, would know. But here the marvellous humour and agnosticism of the hymn confounds us all ...

"This flow of creation, from where it did arise, Whether it was ordered or was not, He, the Observer, in the highest heaven, He alone knows, unless ... He knows it not." [Verse 7]

15

Over a period of several centuries, the Aryans came to have a more settled existence. By 1200 BC, they were ensconced in Middle India [*Madhya Desh*]. At what precise point an elaborate social structure developed, which would henceforth govern the lives of Hindus, is not known; but the *Rig Veda*, which can be dated as far back as 1400–1000 BC, has a famous hymn, *Purusha Sukta*, the "Hymn to Man" (X.90) which describes the origins of the four castes from the Primeval Man.

The Brahmin caste — *I came from His mouth.*

The Kshatriya caste — *From His arms was I made.*

The Vaishya caste — *His thighs produced me.*

The Sudra caste — *His feet gave birth to me.*

The Brahmins, the priestly caste, became the custodians and transmitters of sacred knowledge. They also conducted the rituals to mark the important milestones in a person's life – birth, puberty, marriage and death. The Kshatriyas, or warriors, were charged with the defence of the land, and the duties of kingship and governance. The Vaishyas were the merchant and professional caste. The Sudras served the three upper castes (together known as Dwijas, the "twice-born") and did work considered dirty or degrading.

Some defenders of the caste system (*varnashrama dharma*) argue that the four *varnas*, or social orders, were originally viewed as equal. The entire system rests on the reasonable premise that different people must perform different duties in life.

> Brahmins might have ritual superiority over the other castes, but we were expected to lead lives of indigence.

> Over time the system deteriorated beyond recognition.

> I described the caste system as an excrescence upon Hinduism, and yet I unequivocally asserted my trust in it.

*"**Varna** and **Ashrama** are institutions which have nothing to do with castes ... The calling of a Brahmin – a spiritual teacher – and of a scavenger are equal and their due performance carries equal merit before God and at one time seems to have carried identical reward before man."* Gandhi

An elaborate set of rules, which has considerably loosened in the urban areas of modern India, has governed the relations between the four *varnas*. These rules are set out in the *dharmashastras*, or law books, the best-known of which is *Manusmriti*, "The Laws of Manu".

The sanctity and immutability of *varnashrama dharma*, and, in particular, belief in the ritual and social superiority of Brahmins, were inscribed into the practices of Hinduism.

"Brahmins are 'gods among humans' [manusyadevah]."

"The Brahmin is the Lord of the <u>varnas</u> because of his superiority, the pre-eminence of his origin ..."

MANUSMRITI

Brahmins could not accept food from the lower castes, and especially not from Sudras. An exception was made in the case of uncooked food, such as grains. The rules of commensality were very stringent and the upper castes would not share food with the lower castes. Brahmins employed only Brahmin cooks.

The higher the caste, the greater the risk of pollution ...

Even the shadow of the Sudra, were it to fall upon a Brahmin, would be a source of contamination.

19

In former times, I had to shout "A Sudra is coming!" to warn an upper-caste person of my approach and safeguard his purity.

The Brahmins found us polluting. But that didn't stop them having sexual relations with Sudra women.

Damn this Bhangi.* His touch has polluted me. I'll have to go home and take a bath.

*Bhangi = literally, a dirty person: someone employed to clean toilets, dispose of garbage and do manual scavenging.

Among the lowest of the low are those who have variously been called "Untouchables", "Chandalas", "the depressed classes" and "the scheduled castes". Gandhi called them Harijans, the "Children of God". They describe themselves as Dalits, meaning "Oppressed", and constitute at least 15 per cent of India's population of over one billion. Sometimes the designation "Sudra" includes them, sometimes not.

There is a hierarchy of castes and sub-castes among the Sudras and the Dalits.

Nevertheless, we are united in our opposition to upper-caste Hindu tyranny, since we suffer similar humiliations.

For centuries, we were unable to draw water from the village well.

We were forbidden to enter Hindu temples.

Though the Constitution of India expressly outlaws the practice of untouchability, millions of Sudras and Dalits continue to face acute discrimination. Some Dalit leaders and writers take the view that Dalits are not Hindus at all, while others recognize that Hinduism remains their spiritual and cultural home.

Gandhi endeavoured to open up Hindu temples to Harijans. In this enterprise he was vigorously opposed by the venerated Dalit leader, B.R. Ambedkar, who converted to Buddhism towards the end of his life and encouraged other Dalits to do the same.

Is there then no principle in Hinduism to which all Hindus, no matter what their other differences are, feel bound to render willing obedience? It seems to me there is, and that principle is the principle of caste.

Ambedkar made no distinction between the caste system and *varnashrama dharma*. He viewed caste as the foundation of Hinduism, and rightly recognized that Hinduism has outcast its serfs.

Ambedkar opposed the whole temple entry movement because he saw it as an attempt on the part of Brahminical Hinduism to claim Dalits for themselves and so stultify their aspirations to lead free and dignified lives.

Hinduism is corrupt to the core and is incapable of being reformed.

I would like to be reborn as a bhangi.

This is mere posturing on Mahatmaji's part.

To deny that the Dalits are Hindus is to fail to comprehend that Dalits aspire to equality as Hindus.

Though many younger Dalit writers disavow the designation of Hindus, it is not clear that their views are shared by most Dalit communities. Their gods may be different, but Hinduism has enough shelter of diversity.

23

The real question is the relation of caste to Hinduism. This debate is not easily settled. Many Hindus who belong to the Indian diaspora of the 19th century, in such places as Fiji, Mauritius and Trinidad, claim with *some* justification that caste rules do not inform their practices of Hinduism. Yet, caste does appear to be intrinsic to Hinduism.

Even religions which in India claim to be predicated on a distinct repudiation of caste distinctions, such as Sikhism, Islam and Christianity, show the pervasive influence of caste.

24

To the period from 1000–800 BC, we can ascribe two other developments. The *dharmashastras* or law books describe the life of the Hindu as comprised of four stages (*asramas*). Each stage can be viewed as spanning 25 years.

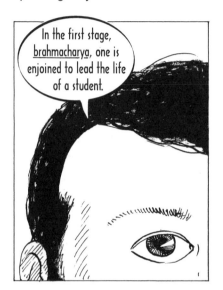

In the first stage, <u>brahmacharya</u>, one is enjoined to lead the life of a student.

Then follows <u>grhastha</u>, where one is engaged in family life and raising children.

The third phase, <u>vanaprastha</u>, is a preparation for retirement and eventual renunciation.

Lastly, one enters into <u>sannyasa</u>, or complete withdrawal from life.

A mechanical view of the four stages obscures more than it reveals.

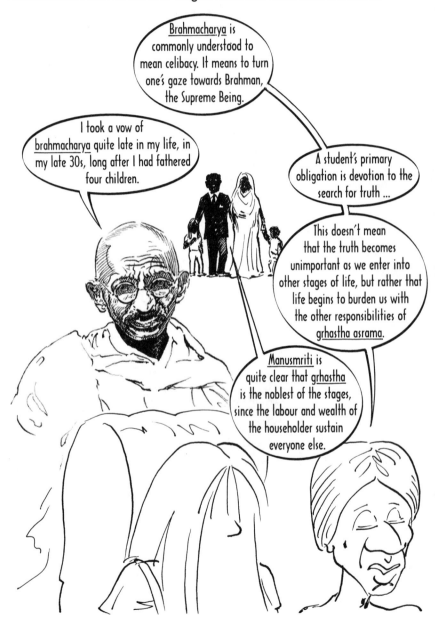

Brahmacharya is commonly understood to mean celibacy. It means to turn one's gaze towards Brahman, the Supreme Being.

I took a vow of brahmacharya quite late in my life, in my late 30s, long after I had fathered four children.

A student's primary obligation is devotion to the search for truth ...

This doesn't mean that the truth becomes unimportant as we enter into other stages of life, but rather that life begins to burden us with the other responsibilities of grhastha asrama.

Manusmriti is quite clear that grhastha is the noblest of the stages, since the labour and wealth of the householder sustain everyone else.

The *sannyasi* is one of Hinduism's best-known figures. To take *sannyasa* means to enter into a stage of renunciation – of wealth, family and the desire for fame. In giving up his attachments to life, the *sannyasi* embraces the entire world as his own.

Hinduism concedes that a younger person may be spiritually and emotionally ready to embrace the stage of <u>sannyasa</u>. Whosoever has developed dispassion can enter into <u>sannyasa</u>.

My view is that a real <u>sannyasi</u> is one who remains very much in this world but is entirely detached ...

What good can anyone do to humanity from a mountain-top?

27

A second development, which can be traced perhaps as far back as 800 BC, is the emergence of a literature collectively known as the Upanishads, viewed as representing the philosophical side of Hinduism. Some of the Upanishads, of which there are 108, may have been composed only a few centuries before the birth of Christ. They were "discovered" by the West in the late 18th century. The philosopher **Arthur Schopenhauer** (1788–1860) described them as the "most rewarding and elevating reading" in the world.

The Upanishads have been the solace of my life and will be of my death.

To every Indian Brahmin today, the Upanishads are what the New Testament is to the Christian.

PAUL DEUSSEN

In fact, the Upanishads are known to relatively few Hindus, whether Brahmins or otherwise.

SCHOPENHAUER

The word "Upanishad" may mean "secret teaching" but is also translated as "sitting near devotedly". The Upanishads call to mind another famous figure of Hinduism, the *guru*. "Guru" now applies to being a master of nearly anything: wine, food, sex, spirituality.

Hindu religious texts, except those of the modern period, almost always existed in the oral tradition before being written down.

Knowledge is transmitted from the guru (teacher) to the shishya (pupil).

The Upanishads may also convey secret teachings imparted to the student.

These teachings are supposed to have been received with utter humility (*sushrusa*), faith (*shraddha*) and veneration for the *guru*, in whose house the pupil would have stayed over several years.

29

It is believed that only Brahmins were entitled to receive the teachings imparted in the Vedas.

"If a Sudra listens to a recitation of the Vedas his ears shall be filled with molten tin or lac. If he recites Vedic texts his tongue shall be cut out ... He who tells religious law to a Sudra and he who teaches him religious observances, he, indeed, together with that Sudra, sinks into the darkness of the hell called *Asamvritta*."

Similar restrictions were placed upon women.

In AD 2000, a group of Indian women publicly burned copies of Manusmriti, declaring that the text was misogynistic.

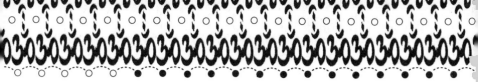

The Upanishads do not unequivocally support the view that neither Sudras nor women could receive the teachings of the Vedas. The *Chandogya Upanishad* tells the famous story of Satyakama. His mother was sexually promiscuous and didn't know who had sired her son. But Satyakama was keen on receiving sacred knowledge and planted himself before the teacher Haridrumata Gautama.

Of what family are you?

I do not know, Sir, of what family I am. I asked my mother. She answered me, "In my youth, when I went about a great deal serving as a maid, I got you."

A non-Brahmin (a-brahmana) would not have admitted this. I will receive you as a pupil. You have not deviated from the truth.

One of the more compelling interlocutors of Yagnavalkya, the most learned of the Brahmins, is a woman by the name of Gargi. She has a relentlessly probing mind and at one point Yagnavalkya says to her:

32

The Upanishads can be described as a meditation on the ultimate nature of reality and the destiny of humankind. What is the nature of reality? How does one differentiate between that which endures and that which is transient? Is there something behind the phenomenal world and the multiplicity of forms?

The Upanishads posit the idea of a unitary, all-pervasive reality which is called Brahman.

Thus the formulaic expression, *neti, neti* : Brahman is "not this, not that". To be fully human means to aim at self-realization, to an understanding of the fact that Brahman, the Universal Soul, and the Atman, or the Individual Soul, are but one and the same thing.

Philosophical dialogues and narratives are deployed to convey the Upanishadic conception of the Brahman and the nature of knowledge. One such story in the *Chandogya Upanishad* (6.1–16) concerns Svetaketu, who spent 12 years immersed in the Vedas and became conceited.

Returning home to his father, Uddalaka, he is put to the test.

> Have you heard of the teaching which enables one to think that which has not been thought of before, and to understand what could not previously be understood?

> What is that teaching?

> By one piece of clay everything made of clay may be known – the modification is merely a verbal distinction, a name; the reality is just "clay" ... so, my dear, is that teaching.

> Place this salt in the water. In the morning come back to me.

When Svetaketu returns the following morning, the salt has dissolved.
Uddalaka has him taste a bit of the water from the top.

Some of the water is thrown away. Svetaketu tastes some from the middle
of the glass.

Svetaketu then takes
a sip from the bottom.

Just as the salt pervades the entire glass of water, so, the Upanishads suggest, a single essence pervades the entire universe. A single seed of a fig, Uddalaka points out, contains within it the essence of all existence. Brahman (universal soul) is none other than Atman (individual soul). Or, in the language of the Upanishad, *Tat Tvam Asi*, "That Art Thou".

Brahman, or Ultimate Reality, is imperishable. This realization gives the wise the fortitude to live.

"The seer sees not death, nor sickness, nor any distress. The seer sees only the All, obtains the All entirely."

[Chandogya Upanishad, 7.26.2]

The Upanishads first gave the doctrine of *maya*. *Maya* is commonly translated as illusion: to take the transient for the permanent is to live under *maya*.

The *Svetasvatara Upanishad* (4.10) describes the Mighty Lord (*Mahesvara*) as an illusion-maker (*mayin*).

Some people mistakenly think of Hinduism as a religion that teaches that the entire world is <u>maya</u> ... Consequently, world-renunciation is the principal objective of human existence.

Since Hindus believe in self-abnegation, and are indifferent to considerations of real life, we'll govern India for them.

37

The doctrine of *maya* became a caricature of Hinduism and a justification for British imperialism in India.

*Maya*, though literally "illusion", means ignorance (*avidya*). A later Hindu philosopher, Shankaracharya, in his commentary on the Upanishads, uses a famous simile to interpret *maya*.

A weary traveller returning home finds something curled up on the road ahead.

In his fear and mental lethargy, he takes it to be a snake.

But moments later, I recognize its true nature.

Knowing the rope to be a rope destroys the illusion (*maya*) that it is a snake.

shankaracharya

Hindu philosophers speak of *maya* as the hugely deceptive glitter of the world. When we are self-realized, or free from *maya*, we understand Brahman as *Saccidananda*: Being (*Sat*), Consciousness (*Cit*) and Bliss (*Ananda*).

Hinduism sometimes goes by the name of Brahminism. Around the time of the middle Upanishads, circa 600 BC, the ritual superiority of Brahmins was clearly established. Brahminism revolved around a multitude of sacrifices. Daily life became too much of a punishing routine over which the Brahmins held sway.

I find the metaphysical speculations of the Upanishads much too abstruse.

The ritualism of the Vedas is tiresome and abhorrent.

Conditions were ripe to draw Hindus, especially non-Brahmins, to other competing faiths and ideologies.

The Buddha (c. 563–483 BC) was born as Siddhartha into a princely family. In his quest for enlightenment, Siddhartha practised in vain the Brahmanic austerities prescribed by renowned spiritual teachers. He then resolved to sit and meditate. In due course, he developed a specific set of teachings known as the Four Noble Truths.

All existence is suffering.

The cause of suffering is ignorance or desire.

Suffering has a cure.

The cure for suffering lies in the eight-fold path of right beliefs, right speech, right conduct, right mode of livelihood, right effort, right-mindedness, right meditation and right aspirations.

The Buddha's contemporary Mahavira (died c. 470 BC) also counselled a simple faith shorn of priests and rituals. Mahavira emphasized right faith, right knowledge and right conduct.

Mahavira became known as Jina or the Conqueror. His disciples came to be called Jainas. There are today several million Jainas, concentrated mainly in western India. Jainas are generally strict vegetarians and famous for their reverence for all living things.

Is there anything common to Buddhism and Jainism? Both religions arose from the soil of India. The Buddha and Mahavira were born into Hindu families. Both religions rejected the caste system, the authority of the Brahmins, the ritualism of the Vedas and abstract thinking.

They can be viewed as practical faiths that also gifted the monastic conception of life to India and so profoundly altered Hinduism.

And let us not forget that Buddhism and especially Jainism introduced vegetarianism into India.

My doctrine of <u>ahimsa</u> or non-violence owes much to the Buddha and Mahavira, its two greatest practitioners.

Another response to Brahminism came in the form of avowedly materialist schools of philosophy. The most notable of these is called Lokayata [from *lok*, meaning people]. The name is telling, since Lokayata refers to the "philosophy of the people".

The Carvakas, or exponents of Lokayata, are known largely through aphorisms such as this one ...

While life remains, let a man live happily; let him feed on <u>ghee</u> even though he runs in debt.

Ghee means clarified butter. It is expensive, and food cooked in it is considered pure and delicious.

This is something of a caricature of Lokayata philosophy. Brahminism condemned Lokayata as the creation of *asuras* (demons). Lokayata is simply described as a form of this-worldliness, an endorsement of the view that the self is nothing but the body.

43

Contrary to the general impression that Hinduism is a religion of negation, renunciation and asceticism, Hinduism insists vigorously on the affirmation of life and the duties of human beings in this life. Imperceptibly, the focus of attention had shifted, in the transition from the Vedas to the Upanishads, Buddhism and Jainism, from the gods to humans. Even as social theorists conceptualized a social order comprising four castes and four stages of life, they articulated the four aims of life (*purusarthas*): *dharma* (moral conduct), *artha* (material wealth) and *kama* (love), collectively known as *trivarga* (group of three), and *moksha* (spiritual emancipation or salvation).

Hinduism is all too often, and mistakenly, identified only with <u>moksha</u> or release from this life.

There is a common image of Hindus flocking to Banaras in search of spiritual freedom.

A class of literature corresponds to each aim of life. The *Arthasastra* (*sastra* = science) of Kautilya, a vast compendium on life in the reign of Chandragupta Maurya in the 4th century BC, is perhaps the best known of such works. A category of works known as *nitisastras*, or manuals on conduct, also belongs to this literature. Here moral lessons are imparted through beast fables.

It seems that my advice on how to win friends was fully anticipated in the <u>Hitopadesa</u>.

HOW TO WIN FRIENDS & INFLUENCE PEOPLE — DALE CARNEGIE

The *Hitopadesa* [*Upadesa* = instruction; *Hita* = advantage: thus, a manual of instructions on how to gain advantage in life], and the better known *Pancatantra*, offer clues on how to outwit enemies, increase wealth, flatter one's superiors, and so on.

Everyone has heard of the *Kama Sutra*, a manual of love-making attributed to Vatsyayana (c. 400–200 BC). It enumerates various sexual positions, the types of love-making, the wiles of women, the rules of courtship and the different characteristics of female and male genitalia.

Some people like to believe that the *Kama Sutra*, Sanskrit love poetry and the erotic Hindu sculpture found at temple complexes like Khajuraho and Puri are striking testimony to the sexual freedom enjoyed by the ancient Hindus.

The *Kama Sutra* is in fact a somewhat dry work, at times rather technical and clinical.

You put your left leg in ...

It offers striking proof of the excessive fondness for categorization among Hindu writers.

ANANGA RANGA ("JOY OF SEX") circa 1500 A.D.

<< There are precisely 243 kinds of "sexual congress", depending, in part, on the length of the lingam (penis) and the width and depth of the yoni (vagina). >>

Long before the *Kama Sutra* was composed, the *Atharva Veda* enumerated the charms to be used to win a woman's love, prevail against a rival woman or regain vitality. Everything points to the fact that Hindus lavished much attention on *kama*.

Many writers have adopted the view that Hindus lost their sexual freedom as they came under the rule of puritanical foreigners.

"In the country of the Kama Sutra, where amorous ecstasy is assimilated to mystic experience, to the perception of the divine that is supreme enjoyment, the puritanism of modern India, arising from Islamic and Anglo-Saxon prejudice, is all the more stupefying ..."

This is the view of Alain Danielou, a French Indologist ...

Whatever the considerable merits of the view that Hindu India at one time prized the erotic life, today such arguments are more likely to be used to paint Islam in harsh colours.

# Dharma: Completing the Triad

If duties are conjoined to privileges, then the pleasure principle must have some constraints. Hindu scriptures and oral teachings prescribe attentiveness to the idea of *dharma*. This is one of the most subtle terms in Hinduism's lexicon: *dharma* connotes moral duty, right conduct, righteousness, adherence to the moral law, and much else.

It is part of one's <u>dharma</u> to venerate one's parents and teachers, to be respectful to one's elders, and to support the needy and the poor.

<u>Dharma</u> also requires fidelity to one's spouse.

In short, <u>dharma</u> means to do the right thing.

But do we always know what the right thing is? Can we say that *dharma* means never to deviate from the truth? What if the truth were calculated to harm someone? How do we know what the truth is?

The slipperiness of *dharma* is marvellously illustrated at nearly every turn in the gigantic epic, *Mahabharata*, which is seven times the length of the *Iliad* and the *Odyssey* put together. Though its earliest portions are dated 400 BC, the nucleus of the story may go back to 1500 BC, around the time of the *Rig Veda*.

49

The *Mahabharata* is the story of the Great War of the Bharat dynasty. Two clans closely related to each other, the Pandavas and the Kauravas [also called Kurus], are drawn into a conflict that engulfs the entire country.

The Pandavas are represented by five brothers led by Yudhisthira; the Kauravas are 100 in number. Yudhisthira has his faults, and the whole story is set into motion by his weakness for gambling; but he is also the paragon of truth, incapable of telling a lie.

50

The Pandavas are represented with much greater sympathy, and eventually emerge victorious, but many of the Kauravas command our respect. One reason why the *Mahabharata* is equivocal in its championing of the Pandavas is that their adherence to *dharma* can be called into question.

51

In the course of the battle, the great warrior Drona inflicts immense damage upon the Pandava army. The Pandavas are at their wits' end, and since Drona seems incapable of being subdued, some strategy is sought to neutralize him. Krishna suggests that Drona would become demoralized if he were falsely informed that his son, Aswatthama, had been killed. Everyone balks at the suggestion; but Yudhisthira accepts.

> I knew that if I were to inform Drona that Aswatthama had been killed, he would not disbelieve me.

> For the sake of <u>dharma</u> it had to be done.

At this point, Bhima, one of the Pandavas, kills an elephant by the name of Aswatthama, and shouts loudly,

> I've killed Aswatthama!

Drona is about to unfurl the Brahmastra, a fierce weapon that could wipe out the entire Pandava army. He hears that Aswatthama had been killed and approaches Yudhisthira.

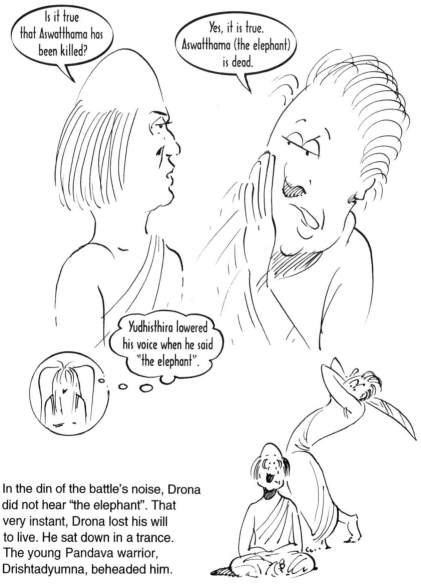

Is it true that Aswatthama has been killed?

Yes, it is true. Aswatthama (the elephant) is dead.

Yudhisthira lowered his voice when he said "the elephant".

In the din of the battle's noise, Drona did not hear "the elephant". That very instant, Drona lost his will to live. He sat down in a trance. The young Pandava warrior, Drishtadyumna, beheaded him.

Yudhisthira did say, "Aswatthama (the elephant)", so he cannot be accused of lying. But he intended to deceive Drona, and some would argue that he stands condemned as a liar. The *Mahabharata*'s narrator prefers to remain agnostic.

Comparatively recent Hindu reformers came to accept the colonial critique that Hinduism had an insufficient conception of ethics. The *Mahabharata* appears to counsel an enormously elastic, even "utilitarian", view of *dharma*. It scarcely helps that Yudhisthira is deviously advised by Krishna.

I have to act in the interest of humanity. When Jayadratha killed the Pandava prince, Abhimanyu, his father Arjuna swore to kill Jayadratha before the sun set the next day.

Jayadratha then went into hiding. I created a false sunset. Jayadratha confidently came out into the open.

An arrow from Arjuna pierced him. The skies brightened again.

Arjuna had taken a vow to kill Jayadratha. He could not be deserted.

Should *dharma* be bound by an intentionalist school of ethics? Or does Hinduism judge actions by their consequences?

Modern social theorists speak about "agency". The debates in the *Mahabharata* also raise important questions about the degree of freedom humans have to undertake actions. Like any other religion, Hinduism advocates truth, fidelity, generosity, love and other virtues, but does not offer a simple set of prescriptions. Hinduism has no Ten Commandments.

55

The *Mahabharata*, in its open-endedness, is a characteristically Hindu and Indian text. However, if it is true that people require models of moral clarity, then we are in a position to understand why, despite its extraordinary popularity, it retains an ambiguous place in the lives of Hindus.

In nearly every part of India, there is a saying that if the <u>Mahabharata</u> is read at home, then a <u>Mahabharata</u> breaks out in one's own home.

When a TV serial on the <u>Mahabharata</u> was telecast over nearly 100 consecutive weeks, everywhere in India the streets were deserted.

The <u>Mahabharata</u> is not a devotional text.

56

The other great Indian epic, the *Ramayana*, occupies a very different place in Hinduism. Not only is its story simpler, but its hero, Rama, is widely idolized, especially in north India, as a ruler, husband and son. Rama is one of the principal deities in Hinduism, and in its "vernacular" versions, the *Ramayana* has a special place in devotional Hinduism.

There is scarcely a Hindu, indeed an Indian, to whom the main outlines of the Ramayana would not be familiar.

The Sanskrit *Ramayana*, attributed to the poet Valmiki, was composed between 400 BC and 300 AD, though here again the kernel of the story is probably much older. Generally, only scholars and people interested in literature read it. And, even in translation, its popularity is vastly exceeded by the *Ramayanas* in various other Indian languages.

Rama is heir-apparent to the throne of Ayodhya, a kingdom in north India. He is the beloved of the people, a devoted son, and has the makings of a benevolent ruler.

However, owing to palace intrigues, he goes into exile for 14 years, accompanied by his brother, Lakshmana, and his wife, Sita.

The abduction of Sita, and the long period of her captivity under Ravana the demon-king, culminate in a hard-fought battle between Rama and Ravana.

Sita is rescued and Rama returns triumphantly to Ayodhya. He is crowned king. There is rejoicing throughout his kingdom.

*The honorific by which Rama would be addressed, especially among devout Hindus: "ji" is a suffix denoting respect, as in Gandhiji, Mahatmaji, etc.

Rama and Sita are viewed as the ideal Hindu couple. It comes as a surprise, then, to learn that Rama eventually responds to the rumours by insisting that Sita undertake a trial by fire (*agnipariksha*). Sita sits on a pile of logs which are set ablaze. She emerges from the fire unscathed. All doubts about her chastity and fidelity are put to rest.

But in the version that I tell, Rama banishes Sita into the forest.

In my version, Sita is deeply wounded by Rama's inability to recognize that she is pure. She leaves Rama and returns to the earth from which she came.*

Notwithstanding his bizarre conduct, Rama is venerated, and Rama and Sita are represented as the perfect example of monogamous marriage.

_____

*Sita means 'furrow'.

Some recent feminist interpretations are extremely critical of the *Ramayana* which is cited as an example of the patriarchal basis of Hinduism. The only conclusion to draw from the fact that Rama and Sita are still viewed as the ideal Hindu couple, despite his mistreatment of her, is that Hinduism expects women to be subservient to men.

But Rama's own justification for his conduct deserves a hearing.

A vicious rumour about my wife was circulated around town. Some of my subjects were deeply suspicious. I found this rumour intolerable.

So I had to be sacrificed?

I never doubted your word and was prepared to swear by your chastity. But, as the ruler of a kingdom, I had to put my subjects before you. I was certain that the <u>agnipariksha</u> would silence the rumour-mongers.

61

That Rama would put his kingdom before his wife may be one reason why he is viewed as a just king by Hindus. The expression "Ramrajya" is heard frequently in Hindi to denote a well-run polity where justice and prosperity reign supreme, much as in Rama's Ayodhya.

I would like to see a modern India run like "Ramrajya".

The fact that there are numerous versions of the *Ramayana* story suggests that many Hindus were unable to reconcile Rama's conduct towards Sita with the representation of him as an ideal husband. Some Hindus have been inclined to view the entire episode of the *agnipariksha* as an interpolation by Hindu patriarchs at a time when Indian society was turning more conservative.

In some versions, Rama and Sita are siblings. No less strikingly, in numerous regional traditions the ten-headed Ravana is represented as the hero. Rama was a kshatriya; Ravana a brahmin. There may also be sectarian reasons for this role reversal. While Rama is an incarnation of Vishnu, Ravana worshipped the god Shiva.

Sometimes Ravana is elevated for loftier reasons. He may represent the traditions of pre-Aryan India in which tribal loyalty was supreme. Ravana was extremely solicitous of the welfare of his kith and kin. His devotion to Shiva was exemplary.

There are many *Ramayanas*, and even *Ramayanas* within *Ramayanas*. The celebrated Indian writer Ananthamurthy speaks of a Kannada version in which Sita insists on accompanying Rama into the forest. Rama refuses.

Life in the forest will be arduous. You are used to the luxuries of palace life.

Back and forth they debate this question. Finally, Sita blurts out ...

In all other versions of the story, I accompany you into the forest. Why cannot I do so in this one?

The self-reflexivity of some Hindu traditions has distinctly postmodern features.

The emergence of Krishna and Rama points to a development that is known by several names and leads to the popular Hinduism that one encounters down to the present day. This development can be termed Sectarian Hinduism, Puranic Hinduism, and even Avataric Hinduism.

The religious literature of the Hindus contains a genre known as the Puranas. Though the *Mahabharata* is known as *itihasa* (history, or literally, "so it happened") and the *Ramayana* is a work of *kavya* (poetry), they are more broadly viewed as one with the Puranas.

Sometime around the beginning of the Christian era, the notion of avatar (<u>incarnation</u>) began to take hold ...

The worship of Shiva, Vishnu and Shakti began to divide the followers of Hinduism.

These changes are best understood through the Puranic literature.

The word "Purana" means old, and the nuclei of some of the Puranas extend to little before the Christian era. In their present form, however, the Puranas date from around AD 250–1500.

By tradition, there are said to be 18 Puranas, but the actual number is much larger. The most authenticated ones include:

**Agni**
**Bhagavata**
**Bhavisya**
**Brahma**
**Brahmanda**
**Brahmavaivarta**
**Brhaddharma**
**Brhannaradiya**
**Devi**
**Devibhagavata**
**Garuda**
**Harivamsa**
**Kalika**
**Kalki**
**Kurma**
**Linga**
**Mahabhagavata**
**Markandeya**
**Matsya**
**Narasimha**
**Padma**
**Samba**
**Siva**
**Skanda**
**Vamana**
**Varaha**
**Vayu**
**Vishnu**

By convention, the Puranas are thought to deal with five subjects ....

The creation of the universe.

Its destruction and renovation.

The genealogy of gods and patriarchs.

The reigns of the different human ancestors.

The history of the Solar and Lunar races of kings.

The Puranas are an immense lore of Hindu myths. They are the scriptures of popular Hinduism, assisting in the transition from Brahminism, and show a receptiveness to folk forms of devotion and worship, as well as everyday arts, crafts and sciences.

The genealogies in the Puranas are such that kings are said to rule for thousands of years. The Puranas also gave rise to the notion of Hinduism as a religion of "330 million" gods and goddesses. The much maligned monsters of Hinduism – ferocious deities with necklaces of skulls around their necks, the cannibalistic-looking demons – proliferate in the playful Puranas.

James Mill, the 19th-century English author of the History of British India:

The literature of the Hindus is fanciful, hyperbolic, and absurd. Tens of thousands of years are described as a mere instant.

What can one expect of those of the Stiff Upper Lip? They seem to read numbers literally. Imagine!

Whatever the classical definition of the subject matter of the Puranas, it would be more accurate to say that some Puranas exhibit devotion largely to Shiva; in others, the devotion to Vishnu predominates. The Hindu Trinity consists of the gods Brahma, Vishnu and Shiva. They are associated, respectively, with creation, preservation and destruction.

It is here that the textbook view of Hinduism fails us. Brahma, by any reckoning, should be just as important as Vishnu and Shiva. But at some point, for unknown reasons, Brahma ceased to be worshipped.

Only one famous temple devoted to Brahma exists in India, at Pushkar (Rajasthan). The Hindus are a practical people. Once Brahma had done his job, there was no further use for him.

pushkar

Though the name Shiva is unknown to the Vedas, he has subsequently been associated with the Vedic storm god, Rudra. He is, even more likely, a pre-Aryan god, since numerous forms of non-Vedic worship characterize the cult of his followers, called Shaivites. This includes practices of asceticism, devotion and the worship of the *lingam* (phallus).

Shiva may have been a fertility god in pre-Aryan India.

One of the many forms in which he appears is Pasupati, Lord of Animals, an image which appears in many Indus Valley seals. His non-Vedic origins may be one reason why he was incorporated into the Hindu pantheon after much hostility and suspicion.

Much as it is with Christian saints, there is an iconography of Hindu gods and goddesses. Shiva is clearly recognized by the trident he holds in one hand, his matted hair, his blue throat, and so on.

*The bull, Nandi, often appears by my side.*

Like all Hindu gods, Shiva is known by many names. He has 1,008 epithets. From the standpoint of Shaivites, Shiva is the Supreme God (Mahesvara), the Lord of the Universe. Nonetheless, he appears in various forms: as Lord of the Cosmic Dance, he is Nataraj; as Lord of Yoga, he is Yogesvara. He is also Shankara (the "Auspicious", the "Beneficent"), Mahayogi (the Great Yogi), and Digambara (the naked ascetic, literally "clothed with the sky").

Wherever in a Hindu place of worship there is a *lingam* (phallus), Shiva presides. The *lingam* is an iconic pillar, rounded at the top. It generally rests in a grooved, circular base symbolic of the vagina (*yoni*). This signifies the generative power of the union of male and female.

However, the <u>lingam</u> is often viewed as <u>swyambhu</u> or self-generated, rather than the work of humankind.

It is also a manifestation of Shiva's cosmic energy.

In place of Shiva, the lingam is installed in most temples in the *garba grha*, the inner sanctum. There is an elaborate ritual for washing and dressing the lingam and adorning it with flowers.

70

The Lingayats, or Virasaivas, a Kannada-speaking caste of South India, furnish a vivid illustration of the veneration extended to the lingam. Their founder, the radical poet Basavanna (b. AD 1106), wrote passionately against the caste system, mocked the Brahmins and preached complete surrender (*bhakti*) to Shiva.

Does it matter how long
a rock soaks in the water:
will it ever grow soft?

Does it matter how long
I've spent in worship,
when the heart is fickle?

Futile as a ghost
I stand guard over hidden gold.
O lord of the meeting rivers.*

Basavanna

*"Lord of the Meeting Rivers" is a translation of *Kudalasangamdeva*, a form of Shiva that was Basavanna's *ishtadevata*, "desired" or personal deity. Hindu families may have a family deity (*kuladevata*), but within the family each person has the freedom to choose his or her own personal deity, or that aspect of the divine which the worshipper finds most appealing.

From Basavanna's own time, it became a common practice for his followers to carry a lingam with them, usually strung around the neck. Even today, at the birth of a child in the Lingayat community, the family priest is sent for, who then proceeds to initiate the infant into the community by ceremonially tying a lingam to the child's body.

The personal lingam, according to the Lingayat community, suggests a far more profound commitment to Shiva than is encountered among those whose familiarity extends only to lingam representations in Shiva temples.

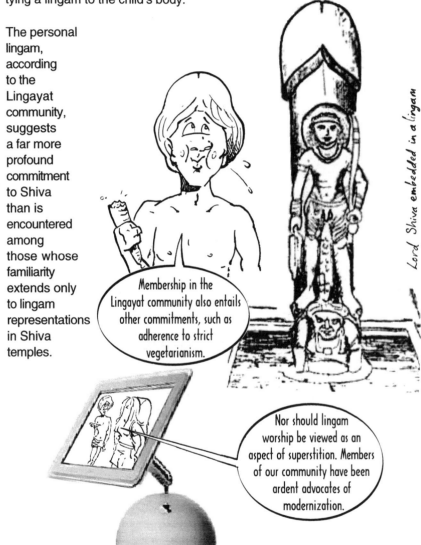

*Lord Shiva embedded in a lingam*

Membership in the Lingayat community also entails other commitments, such as adherence to strict vegetarianism.

Nor should lingam worship be viewed as an aspect of superstition. Members of our community have been ardent advocates of modernization.

One of the more spectacular and at once philosophical representations of Shiva is known as *Ardhanarisvara* (*ardha*=half; *nari*=woman), or God as half male, half female. The right half of the body is male, flat-chested; the left half is a woman with a full, rounded breast, long hair, and an anklet around the foot.

Ardhanarisvara, "God is both male and female; neither male, nor female."

Every man must aspire to be a man but allow the feminine within him fully to flourish. Likewise, every woman must remain womanly while allowing the masculine within her to develop to its fullest potential.

Hinduism's female deities often show signs of extreme ferocity, just as the gods often have feminine characteristics. Hinduism allows much latitude to the idea of androgyny.

Hinduism's deities generally have consorts. Indeed, without his consort, the male deity is incomplete. *Ardhanarisvara* is but the interiorization of the more common form of representation of Shiva and Parvati, side by side. Vishnu, similarly, is paired with Lakshmi, and Brahma with Saraswati.

Hindu goddesses are no mere consorts. Even though Parvati is seldom shown without Shiva, she is worshipped in her own right. In the South Indian city of Madurai, the majestic Meenakshi Sundareshwara Temple honours Parvati, locally known as Meenakshi.

Here I prevail as the regnant deity. People come to worship me. Every evening, at 9.15 p.m., Sundareshwara (my husband, Shiva, the "Beautiful One") comes to lie beside me.

MEENAKSHI

Some might like to view and interpret divine couples as examples for humankind of monogamy. If in Hindu society a woman is seen as nothing if she is without a husband, why should goddesses be exempt?

Parvati, however, represents what might be called *Shakti*, or Cosmic Feminine Energy.

I am not only Shiva's energy, but rather pure dynamism, the very personification of light and illumination.

The origins of Shakta worship lie in the veneration accorded to the goddess in pre-Aryan India. It is sometimes argued that early societies everywhere were matriarchal, but whatever the truth of that sentiment, there is compelling evidence of the cult of Mother in the Indus Valley.

Worship of the goddess (Devi) stands alongside the worship of Vishnu and Shiva as one of the three main strands of popular Hinduism. Moreover, men are just as likely as women to have a goddess as their *ishtadevata*, or personal deity.

Devi appears under numerous names and manifests herself in countless ways.

> Devi appears to me as Lakshmi, the Goddess of Wealth. I invoke her before beginning every new venture.

> I keep a statue of Saraswati, the Goddess of Learning, on my desk.

> The Devi is Amma, Ma, Our Mother, the source and sustainer of all life.

A Hindu woman known simply as Amma has been gathering a worldwide following. Amma's hug is said to have regenerative powers. If asked, a devout Hindu is most likely to describe her as Devi's manifestation.

Hindu goddesses are more frequently worshipped in their ferocious aspect. Durga is the most dynamic representation of Parvati. A portion of the *Markandeya Purana* (AD 250), known as the *Devimahatmya* (AD 550) or *Candipatha*, recounts Durga's exploits.

The demons were on the warpath, and the demon buffalo, Mahisha, was terrorizing the world. The gods were immobilized by fear.

Then Durga, or Candika, came along and offered to lead the counter-attack. Mounted upon a lion, holding the gods' weapons in her hands, she slayed the demon.

Among the epithets by which Durga is known is *Mahishasuramardini*, "Slayer of the demon Mahisha".

Durga's rage is insurmountable and war is her business. Evil cannot withstand her feminine anger.

When Durga's brow grows knotty and black with rage, Kali springs forth from her forehead.

Kali is represented as having a hideous countenance. She is dripping with blood, and encircled with snakes; a necklace of human skulls sits around her neck. With gaping mouth, a lolling tongue, pendulous breasts, she is terrifying and looks ready to devour the world. In this aspect, she is also known as Bhairavi, "The Terrible".

Durga and Kali should not be viewed as minor goddesses. Doubtless, their worship is more prevalent in eastern India, particularly Bengal, an area which was Aryanized and Sanskritized much later than north and central India. But whether as Bhairavi, Camunda or Candi, Devi has a following throughout the country.

One measure of their popularity and significance are the festivals held in their name.

Durga puja is held over ten days during the bright half of the month of Asvina.*

It is a riotous, joyful, grand celebration.

This festival celebrates my manifestation as <u>Mahishasuramardini</u>. To my followers this festival marks my return to my natal home, away from my abode in the Himalayas with my husband, Shiva. Young married women, who pine to see their parents, especially clamour to have my <u>darshan</u>.

---

*This would fall during September–October. There are numerous religious calendars in use in India among Hindus and Muslims.

79

*Darshan* is an all-important notion in popular Hinduism. The devotee is desirous of having a glimpse, a *darshan* (literally, sighting) of the deity. The deity confers blessings; but since the deity is nothing without the devotee, the deity too gets a *darshan* of the devotee.

Large clay images of me as <u>mahishamardini</u> are installed on large platforms, and my devotees bring me offerings ...

On the tenth day, Dusshera, thousands of my images are carried down to the Ganges and immersed in the river. Millions gather to watch this spectacle.

Indeed, everyday worship in Hinduism has something of the ambience of a festival.

I am honoured with the Kalighat temple in Calcutta [Kolkata]. Devotees who especially crave for my blessings, or wish divine intervention to heal a very sick member of their family, each bring me a goat.

The ritually slaughtered goat is then cooked and distributed as <u>prashad</u> (holy food) among my devotees.

80

Just as Lakshmi and Parvati are pan-Indian goddesses, and Shiva, Krishna, Rama and Ganesh are pan-Indian gods, so thousands of deities represent what scholars call the "Little Traditions" of Hinduism.

The various fertility and river goddesses, or goddesses of well-being and disease, are the best illustrations of these "little traditions". Sitala is the Goddess of Smallpox. She is also Mata, the Mother.

SITALA

Does one invoke Sitala to get smallpox?

You're obviously unaware that smallpox was declared eradicated in 1980.

So why should people have a Goddess of Smallpox?

The victim of smallpox was viewed as being possessed by the goddess. Smallpox epidemics are manifestations of Sitala.

81

Sitala is literally the "Cool One". When smallpox strikes a person, the victim has burning pain. Both the victim and the goddess are offered cooling foods. In the Kolkata suburb of Salkia, where an annual festival is held every spring in Sitala's honour, she is taken to the river Hooghly to be cooled in its waters.

Rivers are especially associated with goddesses. The Puranas, as well as the oral and popular traditions of Hinduism around the country, agree that rivers are feminine.

According to the Puranas, these rivers largely originated as <u>apsaras</u>, or nymphs, sent by Indra to seduce ascetics whose growing powers frightened him.

*Dancing Apsaras*

The ascetics cursed the <u>apsaras</u>, turning them into rivers.

Some river goddesses are known only locally and may have nothing of the paraphernalia of worship – images, temples, festivals – associated with deities. Others, such as the famous Ganga, anglicized as Ganges, have an elaborate mythology.

The wide prevalence of goddesses in Hinduism may suggest that the matriarchal basis of Indian society has been overlaid by patriarchalism during the course of three millennia or more.

It is usually assumed that Hindu goddesses are only the consorts of male deities, benign, weak and submissive.

As a general rule, goddesses are married.

But matrimony might also signify the welding together of pre-Aryan traditions (from which the goddesses are largely derived) and Aryan culture.

Yet, this representation of benign married goddesses is controverted by Kali and Durga. Both are husbandless; they are also war-like and aggressive. Many people unfamiliar with Hinduism may be tempted to assimilate the enraged goddess to literary traditions of slighted women. In Congreve's words: "Hell hath no fury like a woman scorned."

Representations of the goddesses are complex. Durga radiates light around her, and is resplendent in her beautiful yellow sari. She is also beneficent: witness her form as Annapurna, "full of food".

Goddesses may show grit. Parvati, determined to marry Shiva, undergoes *tapas*, or asceticism, generally the province and preserve of men. There are also stories of their resistance to domestication.

As the ground was slipping under my feet, I tried to tempt Durga into marriage.

MAHISHA

This was my rejoinder to Mahisha [Vamana Purana 29.36] ...

I may be stubborn, there is desire in my heart, great demon. Only he who conquers me in battle shall be my husband.

Durga

The small fertility and river goddesses, who are usually autochthonous and independent of the pan-Indian traditions, are perhaps the most striking testimony of the persistence of matriarchal traditions within Hinduism.

Vishnu's followers, called Vaishnavas, are at least as numerous as Shiva's devotees. They view him as the Supreme Being, and like Shiva he is known by a thousand names. Vishnu is the Preserver, and, appropriately, he is viewed as representing love, stability and harmony. His consort, Lakshmi (also called Sri), is the Goddess of Prosperity and Beauty.

Lakshmi's colour is red. Hindu brides in Bengal and north India wear a red sari.

VISHNU

Vishnu is distinct in being characterized by his incarnations (*avatars*). It is a particular aspect of Vaishnavism that, in many parts of India, the worship of Vishnu has been eclipsed by the worship of his two most popular incarnations, Rama and Krishna.

Generally translated as "incarnation", the word *avatar* can also be read as "descent". The doctrine of *avatar* retains a pivotal role in Hindu theology and mythology. From time to time, whenever evil or ignorance is on the increase, the Supreme Being must incarnate itself in some form, or descend to earth, so that the forces that stand for good may be reinforced.

When the end of an Age rolls around and time has lost its strength, then Lord Vishnu is born among men.

MATSYA PURANA (47.33)

An *avatar* can also be understood as an exemplar, such as Rama, or as an expression of God's playfulness, wrath, or mere concern for human welfare – and as a warning. The Supreme Being (as Vishnu) might choose to incarnate itself in forms lower than humans, so that what the Greeks called *hubris*, or the pride of man, is checked.

Vishnu is generally held to have ten incarnations, but the number ten is much less "traditional" than is commonly believed. The *Matsya Purana* (47.32–52), for instance, enumerates 12 *avatars*, while the *Garuda Purana* (1.12–35) mentions 22. The *Bhagavata Purana* describes the incarnations of Vishnu as "innumerable, like the rivulets flowing from an inexhaustible lake".

This delicious indeterminacy, endlessly annoying to Britishers in India, is typical of Hinduism and a nightmare for scholars.

Luckily, scholars have to adapt to the religion, however much they may want it the other way.

I first came down in the form of a fish (<u>Matsya</u>) and saved the Vedas from being consumed by the demons (asuras).

I was Vishnu's second incarnation (<u>Kurma</u>).

And I, the Boar (<u>Varaha</u>), followed Kurma. I killed the mighty <u>asura</u>, Hiranyaksha.

According to the *Vishnu Purana*, Hiranyakashipu, the elder brother of Hiranyaksha, practised such immense austerities that the rivers and oceans trembled before him, the volcanoes spit fire, and the astral bodies went astray.

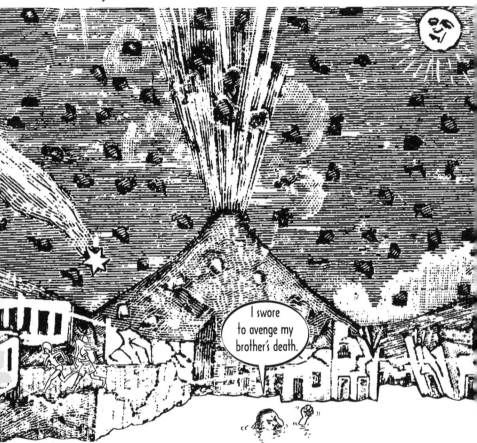

Hiranyakashipu, a Shaivite, subjected his own son, Prahlad, a devotee of Vishnu, to immense pain and suffering. He was keen that Prahlad convert to Shaivism, but Prahlad remained unmoved.

Vishnu decided to put an end to Hiranyakashipu's life. The difficulty was that, owing to his austerities, he had received from Shiva a boon that he could not be killed by humans or animals, during day or night.

Vishnu then resorts to the expedient measure of descending at the hour of twilight as Narasimha, half-man and half-lion, who tears apart the demon king.

It may seem peculiar that the Supreme Being should choose to take such forms as Narasimha, and incomprehensible from the standpoint of ordinary rationality.

But Narasimha points to the animal tendencies within us.

The myth suggests that the enterprise of being human is always fraught with the most hazardous consequences.

We are also reminded that forms of life which we habitually consider below us might have the intimations of divinity. Above all, Narasimha is a metaphor for Hinduism's tolerance for ambiguity. Narasimha represents that moment of liminality in which ignorance is defeated and knowledge vindicated.

Among Vishnu's other avatars, there is, surprisingly, even the Buddha.

Hinduism is often compared to a sponge. Ask me and I'll tell you why.

Whatever happened to you?

By the 12th century, the religion named after me had all but disappeared from the land of its birth. The cunning Brahmins did not treat me as an adversary, but rather made me one of their own.

The Buddha was transformed into Vishnu's ninth incarnation. Appearing as the Buddha, Vishnu encouraged the *asuras* and evil-minded men to reject the caste system and spit on the Vedas, and so effect their own destruction. The Buddhists ceased to exist in India.

We're far from being done with the *avatars*. Hindus say that the final *avatar*, called Kalki, will come at the end of the Kali Yuga.

Umm, I've heard of the Kali Yuga. How does it correspond with our notions of time?

There are four <u>yugas</u> according to our chronologies. The first <u>yuga</u>, or age of the world, lasted 1.728 million years; the present <u>yuga</u>, Kali, will last 432,000 years. We anticipated notions of geological time.

Kalki is represented seated on a white horse, blazing away with a sword that cuts down the wicked and restores purity.

I spend much time with horses. Think of me as Kalki. I'm delivering the world from the wicked. Everywhere evil-minded men should know that I AM the weapon of mass destruction.

George Dubya Bush

We have previously encountered Rama as one of Vishnu's heroic incarnations. Krishna also belongs to the heroic age. But his history is rather more complicated.

Krishna, meaning the "dark one", is the most celebrated deity of Hinduism. The lore around him is nearly inexhaustible. He is one of the central characters in the *Mahabharata*, and the *Harivamsa Purana* chronicles his "life" in detail.

I offered Duryodhana, the Kaurava leader, a choice. He could either have me as god, unarmed, or he could have my army. He chose the latter.

I then became a military aide and spiritual counsellor to the Pandavas.

# Krishna the Charioteer

Krishna's much-debated interventions lead the Pandavas to victory in the Great War. But in the *Mahabharata*, his most memorable role is that of charioteer to the Pandava warrior, Arjuna.

I appear in the guise of a humble human, to put Arjuna at ease. Besides, gods and humans move in each other's worlds.

As the battle is about to begin, Arjuna despairs and throws down his weapons.

Krishna, I see my kinsmen gathered here, wanting war.

My limbs sink, my mouth is parched, my body trembles, the hair bristles on my flesh.

I see omens of chaos, Krishna; I see no good in killing my kinsmen in battle.

Krishna endeavours to persuade Arjuna that, as a *kshatriya* (warrior), his duty is to fight. His teachings to Arjuna are known as the *Bhagavad Gita*, "Song of the Lord". The *Gita* forms part of Book VI (*Bhishmaparvan*) of the *Mahabharata* but it is generally read as an independent work.

Arjuna has a mistaken conception of his *dharma* (duty). His attachments prevent him from having a true understanding of the nature of reality. Krishna's task is to unfold, through the mediating concepts of *dharma* (duty) and *yoga* (discipline), the relationship between *bhakti* (devotion), *jnana* (knowledge) and *karma* (action).

Discipline in action, Krishna is certain, surpasses renunciation of action: "He who performs action without attachment to the fruits of action (*karmaphalam*), and devotes his action to Me, he is dear to Me." (V.3; V.12; IX.26–7; XVIII.2, 9)

Though the teachings of the *Gita* are not in doubt, they lend themselves to many interpretations.

To some Hindus, the *Gita*'s invocation of the *sthita-prajna*, or the person who has cultivated complete equanimity, moved excessively by neither sorrow nor joy, is its most enduring image.

To other Hindus, the *Gita*'s most dramatic moment occurs in Chapter XI. Krishna has been speaking to Arjuna as one human to another, and Arjuna forgets that he is in the presence of the Lord himself. Then occurs the "theophany", as Krishna reveals to Arjuna the true majesty of his form ...

If the light of a thousand suns were to rise in the sky at once, it would be like the light of that great spirit. XI.12

Krishna is very clear that there are three disciplined paths (*yogas*) to achieve union with the Divine or, in the *Gita*'s language, to reach Him.

He recognizes that some prefer to meditate on the Divine. Others will seek the Divine by serving the poor, or selflessly performing their duties (*karma yoga*). Those intellectually gifted are inclined to pursue the path of reason and intellectual discrimination (*jnana yoga*). It is human to be disposed differently towards the search for the transcendent.

In the same way that men love me, they would find my love.

Krishna apparently affirms the multiple paths that lead to him.

Yet he counsels that his devotees (<u>bhaktas</u>) – those who are <u>fixated</u> on Him – are the dearest to him ...

By devotion [<u>bhakti</u>] alone can I, as I really am, be known and seen and entered into, Arjuna.

As Krishna himself says in the *Gita*, though he welcomes those who worship the Supreme Being as the Unmanifested, Imperishable, and Unembodied, ordinary people find a purely abstract conception of the Supreme Being difficult to comprehend (XII.1–5).

*Those who are intent upon Krishna, worship Him with unswerving devotion, they straight away find deliverance.*

*To Krishna's devotees, the <u>Gita</u> is supremely a work of <u>bhakti</u>.*

*Whenever righteousness (<u>dharma</u>) wanes and unrighteousness (<u>adharma</u>) rises, then do I incarnate myself.*

*Krishna is Supreme, yet the <u>Gita</u> explicitly invokes the <u>avatara</u> doctrine, although no one reading it would be thinking of Krishna as Vishnu's incarnation.*

97

The *Gita*'s 700 verses, in 18 short chapters – mirroring the 18 books of the *Mahabharata* – have been viewed, especially in the West, as the pinnacle of Hindu thought.

The Bhagavad Gita is the next greatest philosophical poem to Dante's Divine Comedy, within my experience.

T.S. Eliot

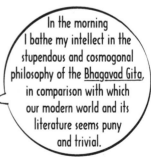

In the morning I bathe my intellect in the stupendous and cosmogonal philosophy of the Bhagavad Gita, in comparison with which our modern world and its literature seems puny and trivial.

Henry David Thoreau

Important as is the Krishna of the *Mahabharata*, and important as is the *Gita* to Krishna's *bhaktas*, the supreme work of Krishna devotional literature is the *Bhagavata Purana*, also known as the *Srimad Bhagavatam*.

The subject matter of the <u>Bhagavatam</u> is the other Krishna of the Indian tradition.

The <u>other</u> Krishna?

The <u>Bhagavatam</u> is mainly interested in the Krishna of myth. This text, especially its Book Ten, lovingly recounts Krishna's childhood in Gokul and the area known as Braj.

In the *Bhagavatam*, Krishna appears as a naughty boy, cowherd, trickster, flirt and lover. His maternal uncle, an evil ruler known as Kansa, had been foretold that Krishna would be the instrument of his death. Kansa, therefore, makes numerous attempts to kill Krishna.

Putana, a female demon

I tried to kill Krishna by feeding him with poisoned breast milk, but he sucked the life out of me.

I took the form of a whirlwind and flew off with Krishna, but he brought me down on the earth with such force that I died.

Trinavarta, another demon

The child Krishna has remarkable prescience. But he also delights everyone with his antics. His foster-mother, Yashoda, is forever hiding the butter of which Krishna is exceedingly fond, but Krishna invariably finds it. Thus he is known as *makhan-chor*, butter-thief.

Above all else, Krishna dallies with the cowherdesses (*gopis*). In countless texts, songs, poems and oral narratives, he appears as the simultaneous lover of 16,000 nubile young women, the man-about-town who frolics with maidens on the village green, the initiator of the *rasalila* or cosmic dance.

One of my favourite antics was to stop by the river where the gopis bathed and steal their clothes.

He beckoned to us from a tree-top and urged us to come out of the water. We were ashamed to do so.

## Erotic Allegory?

Some commentators – and most puritanical scholars – insist that the love of the *gopis* for Krishna must be read allegorically as the love of the human for the divine. A true devotee (*bhakta*) must be prepared to appear before God naked, shorn of the ego (*ahamkara*), reduced to zero.

The *rasalila* completed, Krishna slips away into the darkness for his tryst with Radha.

The *Gitagovinda*, by the Bengali poet Jayadeva (12th century), is an intense work of lyrical eroticism that explores the world of human, sexual and divine love.

Radha and Krishna exchange coy glances, make love, quarrel, and separate. Radha pines for him and recalls their sexual play:

> I fall on the bed of tender ferns; he lies on my breasts forever. I embrace him, kiss him; he clings to me drinking my lips. 2.13

> But what is God without his devotee? Krishna's longing for Radha is not any less intense ...

> He dwells in dense forest wilds,
> Rejecting his luxurious house.
> He tosses on his bed of earth,
> Frantically calling your name.
>   Wildflower-garlanded Krishna
>     Suffers in your desertion, friend. 5.5

It is this Krishna over whom Mirabai went mad, to whom paeans have been sung by millions of Hindus over the centuries, and whose life and loves have sustained the greatest traditions of Indian music, literature and art. This is the other Krishna, the Krishna of the *bhaktas*.

The Bhakti movement originated in the Tamil country in the 6th century AD and, over a millennium, spread to nearly all of India.

The devotional songs of Mirabai, Surdas, Tulsidas, Narsi Mehta, the Alvar poets and Chaitanya remain on the lips of millions of devout Hindus.

The writings of the <u>bhaktas</u> (devotees) possibly represent the largest cache of devotional literature in the world.

Numerous strands went to make up the Bhakti movement. Some bhaktas were Vaishnavas, others chose to worship Shiva. These poets, to whom God appears with a form (saguna), are usually distinguished from nirguna saints (sants), or those to whom God appears as formless.

104

The Bhakti movement can nonetheless be spoken of in the singular because most of its adherents shared certain characteristics.

We rejected ...

- the caste system
- the Vedas as a source of authority
- the growing materialism of Indian society
- the social order of Hindu life
- the sanctity of holy pilgrimage sites
- temple worship
- Brahminical dominance
- and much else ...

Bhakti is to Hinduism as anti-structure is to structure; but bhakti also developed a counter-structure, its own hierarchy of behaviour, belief and emotions. To some bhaktas, veneration for the guru was all-important; others had no guru, but claimed to have received a divine vision.

If Buddhism and Jainism were revolts from outside, the Bhakti poets initiated a revolt from within.

Most of the bhaktas were lower-caste; some were women. Both had been denied access to the Vedas; neither were seen as fit to receive spiritual instruction. Dadu was a cotton carder, Kabir a weaver (*julaha*); Namadev was a tailor, Raidas a *chamar* (leather worker and scavenger).

**Tukaram** (c.1605–49) was born into a sudra family.

I incurred the wrath of the Brahmins when I started composing abhangs,* and that too in Marathi rather than Sanskrit.

Here's an important point. The development of Indian languages is closely linked to bhakti literature. The bhaktas repudiated Sanskrit. They compared it to still water. The vernacular languages, the languages of the people, were construed as flowing bodies of water – expressive, vibrant and fecund.

*abhang* = Marathi metre: another name for Brahman, the absolute, the eternal

106

Tukaram condemned untouchability.

The brahmin who flies into a rage at the touch of a **mahar**
— That's no brahmin.
The only absolution for such a brahmin
Is to die for his own sin.

He who refuses to touch a **chandal**
Has a polluted mind.

Says Tuka, a man is only as chaste
As his own belief.

His sentiments were anticipated in the 15th century by Kabir, who mockingly dismissed Brahmin and Muslim orthodoxy alike in vivid, uncompromising language.

Pandit, think
before you drink
that water!

Pandit, look in your heart for knowledge.
Tell me where untouchability
came from, since you believe in it.

107

The constraints on women were even greater, as the lives of Andal in the 7th century and **Mirabai** (1498–1565) show.

> I refused to be married. From early childhood, I recognized Lord Krishna as my lover.

Andal would marry only Sri Ranganatha, the presiding deity in Srirangam. In *Tiruppavai*, a collection of 30 verses, she imagines herself as one of Krishna's *gopis*.

Mirabai, married forcibly into a great Rajput family, had little interest in her wifely duties. When her husband died, she wouldn't commit ritual sati.

> How could I, when I was married only to Krishna?

> Worldly shame and family custom I have cast to the winds.
> I do not forget the beauty of the Beloved Even for an instant.
> Mira is dyed deeply in the dye of Hari.

Similarly, the Virasaiva poet Mahadeviyakka (12th century) considered herself married to Shiva. Pressured into earthly marriage and domesticity, she expressed her dilemma.

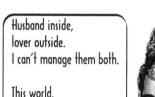

> Husband inside,
> lover outside.
> I can't manage them both.
>
> This world,
> and that other,
> cannot manage them both.

Although the writings of women bhaktas resonate differently, a true bhakta, whether male or female, was expected to approach God as a woman.

> One of the most famous anecdotes from Mirabai's life relates her encounter with a renowned Bengali Vaishnava in Vrindavan, Jiva Goswami ...

> I refuse to meet with her since she is a woman.

> I used to think that the Lord Krishna was the only man in Vrindavan and that all the rest of the inhabitants were gopis. Now I've discovered that there's someone else here besides Lord Krishna who thinks of himself as a man.

The Bengali Vaishnava theologian Rupa Gosvami suggested that one can relate to God in five ways.

> As a mother to her child
> servant to his master
> ordinary human to the Supreme Being
> friend to another friend
> and lover to her beloved.

Kabir, in whose writings medieval bhakti perhaps achieves its apogee, reminds us that some of the bhaktas conceived their relationship to God in yet a different form:

> Pandits read Puranas, Vedas,
> Mullas learn Muhammad's faith.
> Kabir says, both go straight to hell
> if they don't know Ram in every breath.

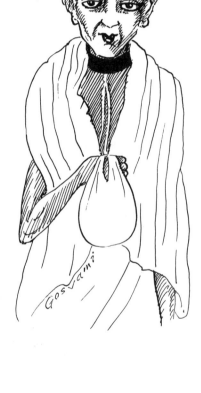

Gosvami

KABIR

Kabir's Ram is not Tulsidas's Rama; nor is it the peculiar formless of the Upanishads. Islam may have helped Kabir in forming his own notion of the formless.

110

# Hinduism in Islamic India

By the 13th century, Islam had established a firm foothold in northern India. Muslims exercised political power until the 18th century.

THE AUTHOR

The history of Hinduism's complex encounters with Islam would be better treated in a comprehensive "Religions of India" volume.

Some vital aspects of this history can be mentioned. Islam's Sufi saints and pirs attracted a large number of followers.

The <u>dargahs</u> [memorials] of Sufi saints in Delhi and Ajmer continue to be places of social interaction between Muslims and Hindus.

Kabir was claimed by both Muslims and Hindus.

In fighting over my remains, and my legacy, they vindicated my belief that adherents of both religions were devoid of true spiritual feeling.

KABIR

Among the *nirguna sants*, **Nanak** (1469–1539) occupies a special place. He preached a simple monotheistic faith, shorn of idolatry and predicated on the equality of all men and women, and emphatically rejected caste Hinduism.

Two stories commonly told about Nanak underscore his repudiation of both institutionalized Hinduism and Islam. The scene is the holy Hindu city of Hardwar ...

I encountered Brahmins who, while standing in the Ganga, were throwing water towards the sun to appease the souls of their ancestors.

I began throwing water in the opposite direction ...

I told the Brahmins that I was watering my fields in the Punjab. They laughed at me. It didn't occur to them that if the water they were sprinkling could reach the sun, then doubtless the water could reach my fields.

112

Nanak also travelled to Mecca. Exhausted and hungry, Nanak fell asleep and was awoken by a Muslim priest.

How dare you sleep with your feet pointing towards the Kaaba?

I invite you to turn your feet to any place where God cannot be found.

At his death, his followers quarrelled. The Hindus wanted to cremate him, the Muslims sought to bury his body.

GURU NANAK,
THE KING OF FAKIRS.
TO THE HINDU A GURU,
TO THE MUSLIM A PIR.

Nanak's teachings would later be institutionalized as the faith known as Sikhism.

The Bauls – or madcaps – are the singing, itinerant bards of Bengal. This sect most likely arose in the 16th century. It drew its members from the lowest strata of Hindu and Muslim society. The religious beliefs of the Bauls drew upon Hinduism, Buddhism and Islam, and bore a marked affinity to the sentiments of the bhakti poets.

> Some wear malas [Hindu rosaries] around their necks, some tasbis [Muslim rosaries], and so people say they've got different religions.
> But do you bear the sign of your religion when you come or when you go?

The Bauls are without customs, conventions or canons. Their *guru* is *sunya*, "emptiness".

> *There's no worship in Mosque or Temple or on special holy day.*
> *At every step I have my Mecca and Kasi [Banaras];*
> *sacred is every moment.*

The great Indian poet Rabindranath Tagore said: "Bauls exemplify the one and only religion, the Religion of Man."

114

By the late 18th century, considerable portions of India had fallen under British rule. The British "discovery" of Hinduism dates from this period.

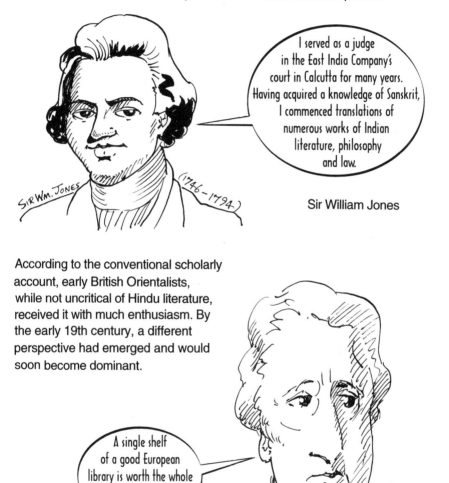

I served as a judge in the East India Company's court in Calcutta for many years. Having acquired a knowledge of Sanskrit, I commenced translations of numerous works of Indian literature, philosophy and law.

Sir William Jones

According to the conventional scholarly account, early British Orientalists, while not uncritical of Hindu literature, received it with much enthusiasm. By the early 19th century, a different perspective had emerged and would soon become dominant.

A single shelf of a good European library is worth the whole native literature of India and Arabia.

Thomas B. Macaulay (1835)

115

The British also drew attention to the barbarous practices alleged to be common among Hindus, such as the rite of *sati* (widow-immolation), human sacrifice, female infanticide, child marriage and prohibitions on the remarriage of widows.

East India Company official:

These practices are sanctioned by Hinduism, an idolatrous, polytheistic faith with monstrous deities. Superstition and tradition have blinded the Hindus.

Sati

A civilization is to be judged by how it treats its women. India is nearly at the bottom of the civilizational scale.

John Stuart Mill

J.S. Mill (1806–73)

The challenge to reform Hinduism was first taken up by **Rammohun Roy** (1772–1833), a Bengali Brahmin.

116

Roy entered into debates with both orthodox Hindus and Christian missionaries. His efforts were largely instrumental in leading the British to abolish sati in the East India Company's territories (1829), and he argued vigorously that the position of women had become degraded in Hindu society. Roy was also a proponent of education in English, since he wished to bring Western scientific and humanistic learning to India.

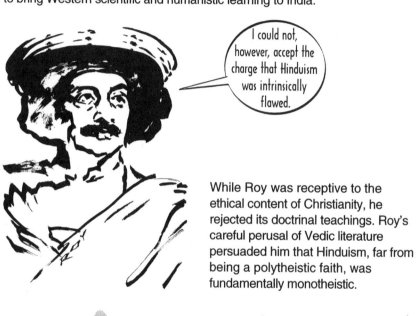

I could not, however, accept the charge that Hinduism was intrinsically flawed.

While Roy was receptive to the ethical content of Christianity, he rejected its doctrinal teachings. Roy's careful perusal of Vedic literature persuaded him that Hinduism, far from being a polytheistic faith, was fundamentally monotheistic.

"Truth is One; Sages Name it Variously"

as is stated in the *Rig Veda* 1.164.46.

117

In 1828, Roy established an organization called the Brahmo Samaj. Members believed in the Worship of One God. Though much later there would be a schism within the Brahmo Samaj, its influence remained profound until relatively recent times. Apart from its advocacy of a simpler, more Unitarian-like form of Hinduism, the Brahmo Samaj promoted modern learning and fought strenuously for the removal of traditional disabilities against women.

In the emergent middle-class Hindu society of Bengal, girls were now educated and child marriages were debated, if not always repudiated.

In western India, a similar organization by the name of Prarthana Samaj (Prayer Society) was established in 1869 by the liberal-minded **Mahadev Govind Ranade** (1842–1901).

Hindu reform movements did not always look to the West, as the example of the Arya Samaj amply demonstrates. Its founder, **Dayananda Saraswati** (1824–83), condemned nearly all developments in post-Vedic Hinduism.

> I hold that the four Vedas are the Word of God. They are absolutely free from error, and are an authority unto themselves.

The Arya Samaj, which attracted a massive following in the Punjab, is generally described as a revivalist movement, but Dayananda thought of himself as a modernist. He argued that no sanction could be found in the Vedas for idol-worship, child marriage, the subjection of women, the practice of untouchability, or any of the other abominations that had crept into Hinduism. The social scientific learning of the West had been anticipated in the Vedas.

Under **Lala Lajpat Rai** (1865–1928), the Arya Samaj mobilized nationalist sentiment against British rule and became a political force in north India. As nationalism gained ground towards the end of the 19th century, Hindu thinkers sought to accommodate Hinduism to their political thinking.

**Bal Gangadhar Tilak** (1856–1920), a Maharashtrian Brahmin, gave support to Dayananda's anti-cow-killing campaign. In a stroke of political genius, Tilak revived both the Ganapati festival and the political memory of Shivaji, a 17th-century Mahratta ruler who opposed the Mughal ruler Aurangzeb, a devout Muslim.

120

Tilak wrote an extensive commentary on the *Bhagavad Gita*.

India's political fortunes will be revived when we understand that the <u>Gita</u> advocates <u>karma</u> yoga, purposeful if desireless action in the world.

The <u>Gita</u> also attracted the attention of <u>Bankimchandra</u> <u>Chatterjee</u> (1838–94), a major Bengali novelist and essayist.

How is it that India fell under the rule of the Muslims and the British?

Hindu India, Bankim was convinced, had cultivated other-worldliness to a fault. He held bhakti and the Samkhya school of Indian philosophy responsible for transforming a vigorous race of Aryans into effete, fatalistic Hindus whose rapturous, ecstatic devotion would do nothing to prevent the subjugation of their faith.

Bankim's *Krsnacaritra*, or *Life of Krishna* (1886), shows an indifference to the Krishna of mythos, and provides an affirmation of Krishna's role in the *Mahabharata*.

121

In Bankim's native Calcutta, one of the most extraordinary figures of modern Hinduism was steering Bengali youth back towards bhakti.

**Sri Ramakrishna Paramhansa** (1836–86), who came from Bengal's backwaters, acquired a tremendous reputation in modernizing, middle-class Bengali families as a Hindu mystic. The growing materialism of Bengali society perhaps attracted educated people to a person who was the very embodiment of sheer spiritual ecstasy.

My devotion to Kali, the Divine Mother, was so intense and sincere that I would remain immersed in <u>samadhi</u>.

This is a state which Hindus describe as transcending all consciousness – paradoxically, also a state of constant awareness, a form of supra-consciousness.

Isherwood

The master liked, above all, to assume the <u>madhura bhava</u>, or the position of the lover as she approaches God. He would dress in feminine attire and imitate feminine behaviour. Blood would ooze from the pores of his skin.

Christopher Isherwood, biographer of Ramakrishna

**Narendra Dutta** (1863–1902) heard both Bankim's call for a muscular Hinduism and Ramakrishna's summons. He responded to both.

As Ramakrishna's principal disciple, Narendra was transformed into Swami Vivekananda. Under that name, he had the singular distinction of both carrying Hinduism to the West, and becoming the torch-bearer of a revived Hinduism that could be embraced by India's youth.

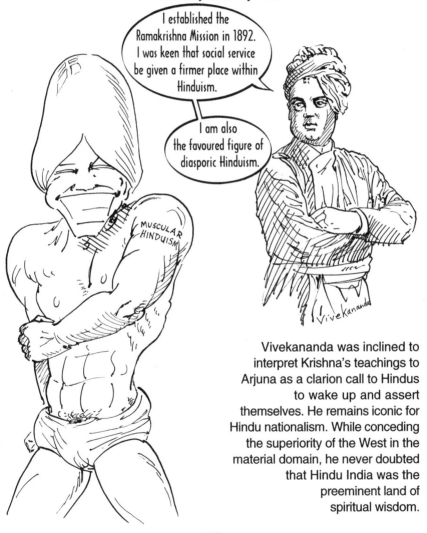

I established the Ramakrishna Mission in 1892. I was keen that social service be given a firmer place within Hinduism.

I am also the favoured figure of diasporic Hinduism.

MUSCULAR HINDUISM

Vivekananda

Vivekananda was inclined to interpret Krishna's teachings to Arjuna as a clarion call to Hindus to wake up and assert themselves. He remains iconic for Hindu nationalism. While conceding the superiority of the West in the material domain, he never doubted that Hindu India was the preeminent land of spiritual wisdom.

123

**\*2 October 1869–30 January 1948**

In Gandhi's own lifetime, people clamoured for his *darshan*. Some claimed he was an *avatar*. At his death, he was said to have become immortal.

As an adult, Gandhi almost never visited a temple. He inaugurated the Bharat Mata [Mother India] temple in Banaras, where in place of a deity there is a map of India.

Whenever a sacred text grates against your conscience, reject the text.

Gandhi is India.

Jawaharlal Nehru

Some Muslims described him as a fervent Hindu nationalist. His assassin called him a foe to the Hindus, and his most virulent critics have dubbed him the "Father of Pakistan".

At his prayer meetings, Gandhi read passages from the *Gita*, the Quran and the Bible. Syncretism, multiculturalism and pluralism are among the many words used to describe his religious outlook.

Gandhi called himself a Hindu, a believer in the *sanatan dharma* (eternal faith). Among the 100 volumes of his writings, this perhaps offers a fair summation of his Hinduism:

*"So, we can only pray, if we are Hindus, not that a Christian should become a Hindu; or if we are Muslims, not that a Hindu, or a Christian should become a Muslim; nor should we even secretly pray that anyone should be converted; but our inmost prayer should be that a Hindu should be a better Hindu, a Muslim a better Muslim, and a Christian a better Christian. That is the fundamental truth of fellowship."*

Gandhi remains a vivid illustration of Hinduism's contention that only a thin line divides gods and humans.

As a living faith which has close to 900 million adherents, there are many interesting questions that arise about Hinduism in the contemporary world.

What can one say about the position of women in Hindu society?

Can Hinduism's resources be utilized in environmentalist causes?

Can the vegetarianism and veneration of the cow found among Hindus be inspiring to others?

Are we in the US just as Hindu as the Hindus in India?

Are Hindu images exclusive to Hindus, or are they the property of the world?

Ganesh

Ganesh, the elephant-headed god, is one of Hinduism's most versatile deities. He is immensely loveable with his rotund belly and generally smiling countenance. Ganesh is the God of Obstacles, and is propitiated at the beginning of any enterprise so that its outcome may be successful.

Vishwa Hindu Parishad, or the World Hindu Council, would claim he is "too versatile". VHP is an organization devoted to the propagation of Hindu cultural ideas, though many of its ideologues have a militant and masculinist conception of Hinduism.

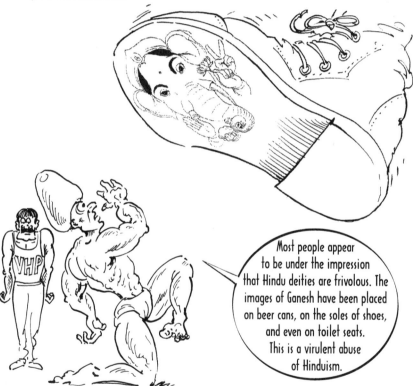

Most people appear to be under the impression that Hindu deities are frivolous. The images of Ganesh have been placed on beer cans, on the soles of shoes, and even on toilet seats. This is a virulent abuse of Hinduism.

As knowledge of India grows around the world, and Bollywood, Indian fashions, Indian classical music, tandoori cooking, and India's famed gurus, among many other phenomena, leave their mark on contemporary world culture, Hinduism will come under increasing scrutiny.

Many Indian feminists contend that Hindu society is hopelessly patriarchal. India, where nearly 80 per cent of the people are Hindus, is one of only a handful of countries where there are fewer females than males, and in the 20th century the female–male ratio declined considerably.

There are 100 million missing women. The neglect of female children and women is a systemic problem in Indian society.

Amartya Sen,
Indian economist

We have to ask whether Hinduism is especially patriarchal, or whether this is a problem that afflicts all religions.

What about patriarchy in Islam, Christianity and Judaism?

It is sometimes argued that the patriarchy prevalent in Semitic religions has a direct bearing on the absence of feminine imagery in these faiths and their inability to conceive of the divine as feminine.

128

Clearly, Hinduism has no dearth of feminine imagery. It is prolific in its representation of goddesses, both benign and ferocious.

One might have thought that the elevated status of goddesses would have beneficial consequences for women.

The new daughter-in-law is often described as Lakshmi entering the house.

But the daughter-in-law in Hindu families is sometimes also harassed for increased dowry. Her life is made miserable, and for the last 20 years, 5,000 women or more have been burned to death each year over their refusal or inability to pay exorbitant dowry.

Some feminists contend that Hindu society has always been patriarchal. One notorious passage is almost always cited in contemporary debates.

In childhood a girl must be subject to her father, in her married state to her husband, and as a widow to her sons; a woman must never be independent.

Manu reading from *Manusmriti* V.148

Though this passage seems unambiguous in its view of women as subordinate, some commentators put a different gloss on it.

As the Mahabharata (1.172.12) suggests, "In a world full of wickedness, it is a great calamity for women to be without protectors."

*Manusmriti*, however, is scarcely alone in expressing these sentiments. Let us see what Tulsidas, the revered poet of popular Hinduism, had to say in the 16th century.

Dhol ganwar shudra pashu nari
Ye sab taadan ke adhikari. (Ramacaritmanas)

The drum, the illiterate, the lower caste, animals and women must be beaten to keep them fit.

But is the evidence from Hindu books conclusive? The same Manu says,

"Where women are honoured, there the gods are pleased; but where they are not so honoured, no sacred rite yields results."

Inferences about the status of contemporary women cannot be easily drawn from Hindu books. It is a species of Orientalism to assume that there is a direct correspondence between texts and the lives of Hindu women.

Many of the debates have crystallized over the rite of widow-immolation known as *sati*. Though commonly used to designate the rite, the word sati itself means "a good wife".

We abolished this inhuman practice in 1829.

The British have no right to interfere with our religious customs. Sanction for <u>sati</u> is to be found in the Vedas.

ROOP KANWAR

Rammohun Roy:

My thorough research in the Hindu scriptures furnishes decisive proof that our ancestors never countenanced such a practice.

132

The debate on sati is far from an academic one. In 1987, a young widow by the name of Roop Kanwar committed sati.

As few as 50 women may have become satis since India acquired independence in 1947. Roop Kanwar, burnt alive on the pyre of her dead husband, was deified as a goddess. Over 100,000 people turned up at her funerary ceremonies. Sati temples attract large followings.

Sati also highlights the problems of widows in Hindu society. Strict taboos on widow remarriage, particularly among Brahmins, have somewhat dissolved.

But the plight of widows is a reflection of the inadequacies of civic reform traditions within Hinduism.

There are some 100,000 of us in the holy city of Banaras alone. We have no means of living except alms.

133

One window into the position of women in Hindu society and into Hinduism more generally is furnished by the commercial Hindi film.

We thought Hollywood was big. But in South Asia, East Africa, the Middle East, Trinidad and elsewhere, Bollywood reigns supreme.

The Indian film industries are prolific. Hundreds of films are made every year in Hindi, Tamil, Telugu, Kannada, Malayalam and other Indian languages.

S. Spielberg

Bollywood Producer

Hindi films, which are immensely popular, are much like Hindu texts condemned by Indian feminists as excessively patriarchal. Though India has a significant population of Muslims, Sikhs and Christians, the films are generally about Hindu society, if seldom self-consciously so.

For several decades, until the 1970s, hagiographies and a genre known as "mythologicals" were common in Hindi and regional cinemas. Among the former, there are famous films on the saints Tukaram (1936) and Dnyaneshwar (1940).

> Several films have been made on me. The first was in 1933, but the most memorable version (<u>Meera</u>) appeared in 1945. M.S. Subbulakshmi's renderings of my <u>bhajans</u> are dear to me.

Mirabai

> The very first film in Gujarati in 1932 was made on me.

Narasimha Mehta, 15th-century Gujarati *bhakta*

> This film was released less than two years after Gandhi's famous salt march.

> Along the way, my companions and I sang Narsi Mehta's profoundly moving <u>bhajan</u>.

> Vaishnav Jan To Teine Kahiye Je Peer Parai Jane Re.

> He only can be called a Vaishnava who feels the sufferings of others as his own.

The *Ramayana*, *Mahabharata* and Puranas were fodder for the "mythological". The film *Subhadra* (Hindi/1946) dramatized the disagreement between Krishna and his stepbrother Balarama over the marriage of their sister Subhadra. *Shri Krishnavataram* (Telugu/Tamil, 1967) recounted major episodes from Krishna's life. The list is endless.

I played the role of gods so often that my fans mistook me for a god.

N.T. Rama Rao, famous Telugu movie star turned politician

The mythological *Jai Santoshi Maa* (1975) had an extraordinary impact. The wives of Vishnu, Brahma and Shiva put a woman called Satyavati, who is a fervent earthly devotee of the goddess Santoshi, to numerous tests. Their intent is to make her life miserable so that her faith in Santoshi falters. Though Satyavati is temporarily separated from her husband, tormented by her sisters-in-law, and nearly raped, Santoshi Maa invariably comes to her rescue. Satyavati's faith in Santoshi remains unbroken, and the goddess is accepted into the pantheon.

137

With its garish sets and crude special effects, *Jai Santoshi Maa* appears to exemplify popular, devotional Hinduism.

Gods and Goddesses are born regularly in South Asia. Often they invade our personal life or enter it as our guests ... no wide chasm separates the gods and motivations of gods and that of the humans.

Santoshi

Nandy

Ashis Nandy, Indian critical theorist

The world of the gods is not unlike that of humans.

They quarrel and experience sexual jealousy.

The film deliberately sets up an overt contrast between "High Hinduism" and folk Hinduism. Lakshmi, Parvati and Saraswati are well-fed and lead opulent lives, but Santoshi Maa is content with offerings of *gur-chana* (cane sugar and chickpeas), food consumed by the poor.

*Jai Santoshi Maa* opens up the possibility that goddesses as well as ordinary women inhabit what might be called an autonomous domain. Gods and males play a relatively minor role in the film, and Satyavati herself accomplishes her integration into the family much as Santoshi fights with determination to win a place in the divine pantheon.

138

Mythologicals aside, the popular Hindi film opens windows into Hindu culture at nearly every turn. The film director Manmohan Desai (1936–94), noted for his blockbusters *Amar Akbar Anthony* (1977), *Coolie* (1983) and *Mard* (1985), stated:

ALL my films are about the <u>Mahabharata</u>.

The Hindi film is firmly grounded in the mythic world of Hinduism. Sometimes this is done quite subtly, as in Shyam Benegal's retelling of the *Mahabharata* story (*Kalyug*, "The Machine Age", 1980), where two industrial families, the Puranchands and Khubchands, enter into a bitter feud.

Often the director makes not the slightest attempt to disguise the Puranic inspiration for his story.

Cinema viewers might recognize <u>Hum Paanch</u> ["We Five", Hindi/1980] as a film which derives its story from the <u>Mahabharata</u>.

The five Pandava brothers encounter evil in the form of the landlord Veer Pratap Singh (Duryodhana, the oldest of the Kauravas) and his sidekick Lala (Shakuni, the scheming uncle who leads the Kauravas to perdition).

139

Even films that seldom come to mind in thinking of Hinduism can easily be summoned as instances of Bollywood's encounter with the Hindu world.

In the immensely popular film *Dilwale Dulhaniya Le Jayenge* ("The Bravehearted Will Carry the Bride", 1995), the heroine, Simran, undertakes the *Karwa Chauth*, a fast almost universally observed by married Hindu women in north India for the long life of their husbands.

Though my parents had betrothed me to someone other than my lover, I was determined to hold fast to my dreams. So I undertook the fast in honour of the man whom I had already wed in my imagination.

In the film Guddi I play a teenaged girl who has a crush on the filmstar Dharmendra. My love for him was akin to the love that Mirabai had for Krishna.

140

As ubiquitous in any Indian town as the gigantic, hand-painted billboards advertising Hindi films are the cows on the streets.

There is a widespread impression that vegetarianism is an intrinsic aspect of Hinduism. Both Islam and Judaism view the pig as an unclean animal and prohibit the consumption of pork.

Hinduism appears unique in both its veneration for the cow and prohibiting the consumption of beef.

Every Hindu I have ever encountered won't touch beef.

And the Brahmins known to me are fanatic about their vegetarianism.

In actual fact, only a small minority of Hindus is vegetarian. While it is generally true that the taboo on eating meat is far more likely to be followed by Brahmins than by lower-caste Hindus, not all Brahmins are vegetarians. Kashmiri Brahmins (known as Pandits) are renowned for their lamb delicacies; Bengalis, whether Brahmins or otherwise, take to fish as fish do to water.

But it is generally true that the diet of the average Hindu is much more likely to be vegetarian than non-vegetarian.

Indian cuisines are much more accommodating to vegetarian tastes than those of other nations.

As a vegetarian, I find that Indian restaurants are among the very few that have fully fledged vegetarian menus.

Though evangelical-minded Hindus (something of an oxymoron) cherish the fond belief that a growing interest in vegetarianism in the West signifies a new-found interest in Hinduism, the growing number of vegetarians in Europe, the United States and elsewhere have displayed no particular proclivity towards Hinduism.

Where did the association between Hinduism and vegetarianism arise? Does Hinduism shed some light on the origins of vegetarianism and the outlook of its adherents?

Unlike the Indus Valley people, who were agriculturists and traders, the Aryans were a pastoral people and slaughtered cattle as food.

The emphasis placed on *ahimsa* (non-violence) by both the Buddha and Mahavira first furnished the impetus to turn towards vegetarianism. The Buddha himself, however, partook of pork for his last meal, and the precepts of *ahimsa* were taken much further by Mahavira's Jaina followers.

MAHAVIRA

*Our Jaina ancestors gave up agriculture so that no living creature would come under their plough. They took to trading and business.*

Even today, the vast bulk of Jainas remain devoted vegetarians. In Gandhi's native Gujarat, where the Jainas exercised a profound influence upon Hindus, devout Hindu families also embraced vegetarianism. Historically, the upper castes, who found members of their community deserting the "Hindu" fold for Buddhism or Jainism, increasingly came to adopt vegetarianism.

K.M. Munshi,
patriotic Hindu writer

*In spite of Jainism and Buddhism, fish and meat, not excluding beef, were consumed extensively by the people.*

Munshi

144

The veneration for the cow, then, dates to some period *after* Buddhism and Jainism were introduced to India. The cow was used to till the land and transport goods and people, but in the Puranas it is clearly symbolic of well-being, wealth and prosperity. Its milk nurtured humankind: thus the notion of "*gai mata*", the cow as mother of all. The Puranas also invoke the idea of *Kamadhenu*, "the wish-granting cow".

Though early law books, such as the <u>Apastamaba Dharma Sastra</u>, permitted the consumption of beef, by the 4th century BC the moral prohibition on the killing of cows was well in place.

The killing of a cow (<u>go-hatya</u>) is a most serious crime.

Kautilya, author of *Arthasastra*

Around this time, it probably became a common practice to require Hindus to imbibe the five products (*panch gavya*) of the cow, namely milk, ghee, curds, urine and dung, as an atonement for wrong-doing.

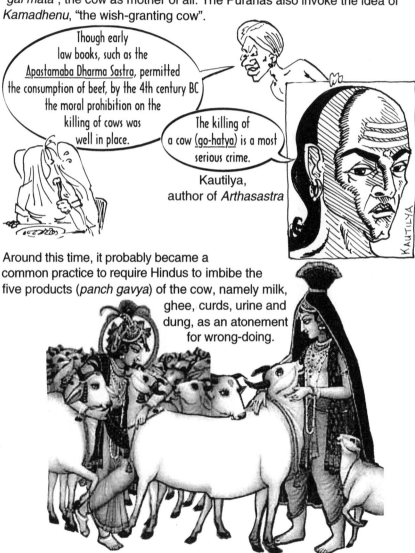

With the coming of Islam to India, the veneration of the cow among Hindus likely increased. Muslims slaughtered the cow at religious festivals, a practice calculated to strengthen the Hindu resolve to demand protection for the cow. The sentiment sometimes encountered among orthodox Hindus that Muslims and low-caste Hindus are "unclean" stems from the fact that these groups work in the tanning and leather industries.

The cow's natural products are sacred to orthodox Hindus, but leather products from cow hide are defiling.

The association of Muslims with leather industries is certainly one aspect of the social segregation between Hindus and Muslims.

Muslims eat the cow, Hindus worship it. Can two people be more unlike each other?

146

During the colonial period, there was a marked increase in religious conflicts over the cow. Hindu nationalists formed cow-protection leagues, and though Gandhi unequivocally condemned the violence that accompanied efforts to induce Muslims to give up cow slaughter, he described cow protection as an "ennobling creed". Gandhi declared:

> No one who does not believe in cow-protection can possibly be a Hindu.

At the same time, many Indian nationalists were also persuaded that vegetarianism had rendered the Hindu effeminate.

> I wrote in my autobiography that when I was growing up, a doggerel by the Gujarati poet Narmad was much in vogue ...

> Behold the mighty Englishman
> He rules the Indian small,
> Because being a meat-eater
> He is five cubits tall.

> Beef, biceps and the Bhagavad Gita shall be India's salvation.

Swami Vivekananda

147

The veneration for cows still remains Hinduism's most visible characteristic. There is no nationwide ban on cow slaughter, but it is prohibited in some states and cow-protection has constitutional sanction: *Article 48: "The State shall endeavour to ... take steps for ... prohibiting the slaughter of cows and calves and other milch and draught cattle."*

In late 2002, five young Dalit men were lynched by upper-caste Hindus who caught them skinning a cow.

In Hindu India, the death of a cow is more likely to earn one an informal death sentence at the hands of a mob than the killing of a person.

Robert Trumbull, the *New York Times* correspondent in India during the Second World War, reported that: "American servicemen in Calcutta were instructed that if a traffic situation arose in which the driver had a choice of striking a cow or a human, hit the human and proceed without stopping to a police station."

When the "mad cow" (BSE) disease struck Britain and hundreds of thousands of cows were killed and burnt, many Hindus were horrified.

We suggested that these mad cows be shipped to India. No, we're not mad: we have the world's largest cattle population. What's another million or two head of cattle?

Last year we won a $10 million lawsuit against McDonald's since it misleadingly advertised its french fries as vegetarian food.

McDonald's in India is unable to sell its trademark Big Mac or other beefburgers. This, however, is not merely a concession to the sentiments of Hindus, but an occasion for McDonald's to portray itself as a multicultural corporation with a "caring" ethos.

149

It is no exaggeration, then, to say that vegetarianism for some Hindus is their dharma.

If dharma also signifies a moral awareness of the world around one, shouldn't we ask whether Hinduism's veneration for the cow extends to nature in general?

Vegetarianism shows an ethical responsibility towards the world. People wouldn't be starving if we were not using so much land to grow food to fatten cattle.

The Hindu gods have mountains as their abode, the rivers are viewed as goddesses, and the sacredness of water is signified by the tanks of water found in traditional Hindu temples. Hinduism, it stands to reason, is a religion that should be enlisted in environmental causes.

Yet every study shows that the vast bulk of India's rivers and other bodies of water are terribly polluted, none more so than the Ganga. So holy is the Ganga that many devout Hindus store a bottle of Ganga *jal* (water) in their homes.

We believe that administering Ganga jal to a dying person washes away his sins and gives him mukti [deliverance].

Giving me Ganga jal will certainly ensure my speedy death!

At places such as Banaras, the Ganga is nearly black from sewage and human waste. Hundreds of millions of images have been immersed over the years into bodies of water during Durga Puja and Ganesh Chaturthi. How many Hindus ever gave any thought to the environmental consequences of these actions?

151

If environmental disasters litter the Indian landscape, it is also true that common people have fruitfully used the spiritual and cultural resources of Hinduism to safeguard their natural inheritance.

The Chipko movement, in the Garhwal region of north India, saw the mobilization of village women alarmed at the rapid rate of deforestation due to the commercialization of logging.

*When the contractors arrived to cut down the trees, we formed a chain and hugged the trees.*

*What do the forests bear? Soil, water and pure air?*

*The Chipko women symbolized the forest as Vana Durga, the earth mother and tree goddess.*

Vandana Shiva, leading ecofeminist

The Bishnoi live largely in Rajasthan. They have lately drawn attention as an example of people who for generations have been practising environmental conservation, holistic science, and what today would be termed wise resource management.

The founder of this community, Jambaji (c. 1451–c.1537), counselled compassion for all living beings, demanded complete adherence to non-violence and advocated vegetarianism. Though the Bishnois worshipped Vishnu, they adopted the Muslim practice of burial of the dead.

Jambaji could not countenance the idea of felling a tree to obtain wood for the funeral pyre.

The black buck and Indian gazelle continue to roam freely in the areas inhabited by the Bishnoi.

The future of mother earth looks good in the hands of the Bishnoi and other similar communities.

Perhaps some 15 million Hindus, excluding the Hindu populations of Nepal and Bali, live outside India. Small as is the number, there is scarcely any country where Hindus have not established something of a presence.

An earlier generation of middle-class children in India grew up on *Amar Chitra Katha* comics. The brightly coloured drawings breathed life into the heroes of the *Mahabharata*, the *Ramayana* and the Puranic myths.

The dozens of titles in this series anticipated the more recent "commercialization" of the epics and Puranic myths. Ramanand Sagar's epic TV serials, *Ramayana* (1986–8) and *Krishna* (1989) brought the Puranic literature to television screens. B.R. Chopra followed with the *Mahabharata* (1988–90).

Sagar's Ramayana homogenized the narrative. It elevated to supreme status the <u>Ramacaritmanas</u> of Tulsidas.

Sagar's Sita is flat and one-dimensional. She embodies the docility and submissiveness prized by Hindu males.

One of the World's Greatest Epics

MAHABHARAT

A WORLD RECORD

WORLD'S MOST VIEWED MYTHOLOGICAL SERIAL

155

# The Internet and Hinduism

Cyberspace and Hinduism appear to have been made for each other. Both are decentred, polyphonic and polymorphous. The web is just as hard to regulate as Hinduism, which has no founder, no supreme doctrinal authority, no precise place of origin.

Some Hindus have taken avidly to cyberspace in an endeavour to correct the false impressions about Hinduism entertained by the outside world. They have generated what might be called new histories of Hinduism. One of their pet theories is that there never were Aryan migrations to India.

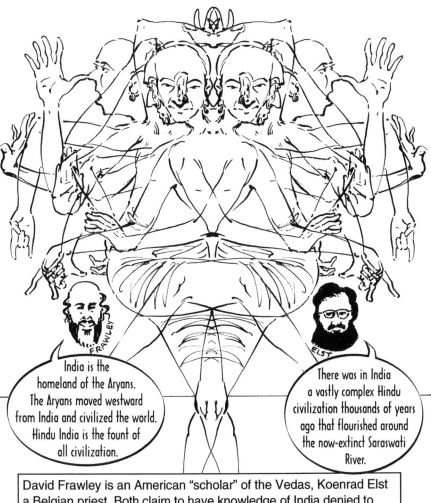

India is the homeland of the Aryans. The Aryans moved westward from India and civilized the world. Hindu India is the fount of all civilization.

There was in India a vastly complex Hindu civilization thousands of years ago that flourished around the now-extinct Saraswati River.

David Frawley is an American "scholar" of the Vedas, Koenrad Elst a Belgian priest. Both claim to have knowledge of India denied to the Hindus themselves. Talk of out-Hinduing the Hindu!

Nowhere are these new Hindu histories being generated with greater vigour than in the United States. Many of these neophyte "historians" of India and Hinduism are computer professionals and scientists who believe that their occupational work makes them more capable of having regard for objectivity and scientific "truth".

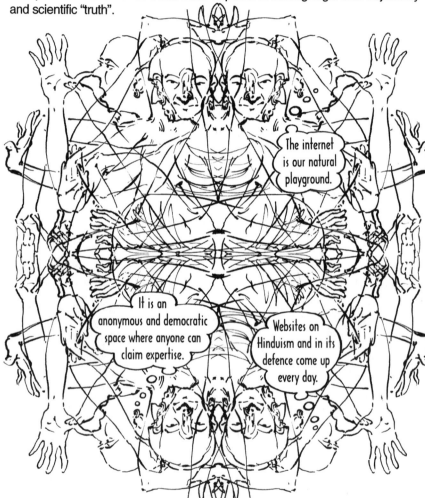

The internet is our natural playground.

It is an anonymous and democratic space where anyone can claim expertise.

Websites on Hinduism and in its defence come up every day.

One website features the Hindu Holocaust Museum to document what is alleged to be the murder of millions of Hindus by Muslim invaders. Websites on Hinduism document Islamic terrorism, a decisive sign that Islam is critical to Hindu self-identity.

Some Hindus in the Indian diaspora see themselves as the vanguard of a revived, dynamic, militant form of Hinduism. They are proud to be Hindus, but not always proud to be Indians.

The Indian (largely Hindu) community in the US is extremely affluent. There is considerable evidence that revivalist forms of Hinduism, as well as political organizations promoting militant Hinduism, have received support from US-based Hindus.

The community has also supported the construction of hundreds of new temples, some costing millions of dollars.

I was sent to the Sri Venkateswara temple in Seven Hills outside Pittsburgh to sculpt images of Hindu deities.

Craftsman from Chennai

But the Indian diaspora extends well beyond the US. In the older, 19th-century Indian diaspora of Fiji, Mauritius, Guyana, Surinam, South Africa and Trinidad, Hinduism has flourished without acquiring the aggressive overtones commonly encountered among its adherents in the US, Britain and other post-industrial nations.

Much less is known about the vibrant Hindu communities of the "under-developed" world.

Using the Puranic form of literature, I wrote the first Purana outside India. The Dauka Puran, in 2000, was the first such book ever written in Bhojpuri.

Subramani
(Indo-Fijian writer)

The Hindus of Trinidad have retained certain forms of religious music that have all but vanished in India. We also created a form of music called "Chutney".

We might even call Java, which is nearly 100 per cent Muslim, part of a Hindu diaspora. Javanese puppet plays, dances and narrative traditions draw nearly all their stories from the *Ramayana*, *Mahabharata* and Puranas. The Hinduism encountered there displays all the vibrancy and strength of the religion's profoundly moving aesthetic, cultural and

Secular Indians and many others with a humanist vision think of the future of India as bleak. The country is now governed by an alliance of parties headed by the Bharatiya Janata Party (BJP), and though the BJP has not openly declared its desire to turn India into a Hindu state, the party vigorously seeks to promote the interests of Hindus.

In early 2002, following an attack upon a train carrying supporters of Hindu organizations in which nearly 60 Hindus lost their lives, the entire state of Gujarat was ransomed to Hindu mobs that tore into Muslim communities and killed at least 2,000 Muslims.

Narendra Modi, Gujarat's Chief Minister

161

Gujarat is the native state of Mahatma Gandhi. At Sabarmati Ashram in Ahmedabad, from which Gandhi led a nation to independence, Muslims fleeing the violence were turned away. Nearly 90 years before, shortly after Sabarmati Ashram was founded, Gandhi admitted a Dalit family.

A worker at the ashram objected to the admission of a Dalit family.

Our donor decided to withdraw all funds from the ashram.

We had a crisis on our hands. But we decided to remain firm.

An anonymous donor drove up and handed over a large sum of cash to Gandhi.

An ashram is a retreat, a hermitage where Hindus go to find solace from the weariness of the world. Students at ashrams were instructed by their gurus in the Vedas and *sastric* literature. In a stroke of brilliance, Gandhi revived an ancient religious institution and transfused it with new meaning.

The Hindu conception of the social order has always accorded religious supremacy to the Brahmin and political authority to the Kshatriya. The Brahmin and the Kshatriya complement each other. Gandhi's position is familiar to Hindus.

163

The militant Hindu's conception of the admixture of politics and religion has absolutely nothing in common with Gandhi's worldview.

I sought to infuse Hinduism with a new sense of political awareness and ethical responsibility in a troubled world.

Though Gandhi was a deeply religious man, and a staunch advocate of Hinduism, he understood that spiritual emancipation could be achieved only in the slum of politics.

Hindu militants who wield political power, and their supporters, have a vastly different conception of Hinduism.

VHP

164

They prefer not to call their faith Hinduism but would rather use the word "Hindutva". In fact, they despise Hinduism as well as Hinduism's greatest figure in the modern period, Mohandas Gandhi (aka Mahatma=great soul).

The word "Hindutva" was used by Vinayak Savarkar, a Hindu patriot later charged with conspiring to murder Gandhi.

I dislike the word Hinduism. It is of foreign origin. Hinduism is a chaotic faith. Hindutva denotes the essence of Hinduism.

Savarkar

Hinduism must be pared down to its essentials. Hindutva does so.

VHP

HINDUTVA

On 30 January 1948, Nathuram Godse, a Maharashtrian Brahmin, assassinated Gandhi. Godse had been associated with numerous organizations advocating Hindu supremacy, including the Hindu Mahasabha. At his trial, Godse offered an elaborate defence of his actions. Invoking Krishna's teachings to Arjuna, he described the killing as the performance of his duty.

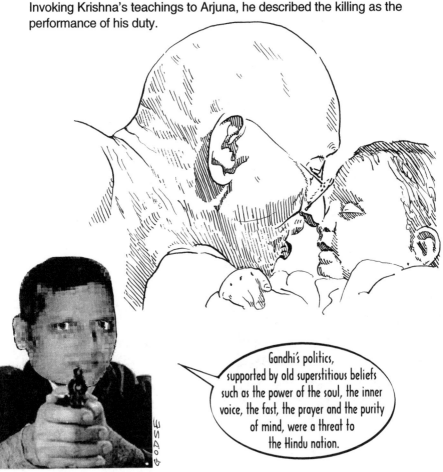

Gandhi's politics, supported by old superstitious beliefs such as the power of the soul, the inner voice, the fast, the prayer and the purity of mind, were a threat to the Hindu nation.

Gandhi's doctrine of non-violence (*ahimsa*), Godse argued, had emasculated Hindus and stripped them of the weapons and resolve to fight invaders and usurpers. A Gandhian-style politics was calculated to earn derision from the world. India would never become a proper nation-state. The old man was an obstacle.

# Bajrang Dal: Debasing Hinduism

The Bajrang Dal is the most chilling example of a Hindu organization that, while charging itself with the task of defending Hinduism, has trashed the faith. Bajrang Dal means "Army of Hanuman".

In traditional iconography, Hanuman sits at the feet of Rama and Sita and looks up to them with adoration and humility. He is also the very personification of learning, courage, strength and selfless service. The *Ramayana* describes him as peerless.

> Hanuman, the Monkey God, assisted me in defeating Ravana and recovering Sita.

Rama

"Peerless", too, is the Bajrang Dal. They have terrorized Muslims, Christians, lower-caste Hindus and (in their language) "pseudo-secularists". Their website, www.hinduunity.org, literally exhorts Hindus to help in exterminating Islam.

The Bajrang Dal shows that Hindutva has nothing to do with Hinduism, but only with the exercise of power.

167

On 6 December 1992, the Babri Masjid, a 16th-century mosque in the north-Indian city of Ayodhya, was reduced to rubble by a large crowd numbering in the thousands. Many commentators described it as India's darkest hour since independence in 1947. It was also one of Hinduism's saddest days.

The Babri Masjid stood at the exact spot where Lord Rama was born. The mosque was built by destroying the temple.

Some historians at Jawaharlal Nehru University, Delhi, did not agree ...

One historical wrong cannot be corrected by another wrong.

Hindus are only reclaiming what was theirs. The Babri Masjid could not be allowed to stand as a perpetual reminder to the Hindus of their humiliation under Muslim rulers.

The advocates of Hindutva are animated by a feverish sense of history. The now-destroyed Babri Masjid is described by Hindutva ideologues and their supporters as *Ramjanmabhoomi*, the earth where Rama's birth took place, or also *Ramjanmasthan* (the place where Rama was born).

The evidence provided in support of this claim is absolutely negligible.

We are now told with certainty that Rama was born in 7238 BC ... 8524 BC ... at 8.27 a.m. ...

But supposing it were true?

No Hindu, until comparatively recent times, ever considered it supremely important to establish the historicity of Rama. The same can be said with respect to Krishna.

169

More than any other major faith in the world, Hinduism is a religion of mythos, a "story-telling" faith.

I wanna tell you a story...

Hindu Ascetic

Does this mean that Hinduism is entirely fictive? That it has no history?

Hinduism doubtless has a history. One can chart with some certainty the historical evolution of Hinduism.

170

But to say that Hinduism is largely a religion of mythos, rather than of history, is to suggest that the historical mode of thinking has never much interested Hindus. The beauty, genius and strength of Hinduism reside in its indifference to attempts to historicize its deities, furnish it with a historical founder, or turn it into a more manageable religion.

Would Hinduism be any more attractive if conclusive proof of the historicity of Krishna and Rama were put on offer today?

There's a stereotype behind me.

Should Banaras be turned into the Kaaba* of Hinduism?

Or is it not enough to believe that any water used in a temple becomes transformed into the sacred water of the Ganges?

*Kaaba—The House of Allah

If Hinduism is to emerge resilient and resplendent, it shall have to be safeguarded from those who posture as its most vigorous defenders.

# Further Reading

Among scholarly introductions to Hinduism, the best are T.M.P. Mahadevan, *Outlines of Hinduism* (Bombay: Chetna, 1971); Klaus Klostermaier, *A Survey of Hinduism* (New York: State University of New York Press, 1989); and especially Julius Lipner, *Hindus: Their Religious Beliefs and Practices* (London: Routledge, 1994). More encyclopaedic are Heinrich Zimmer, *Philosophies of India* (London: Routledge, 1951) and Benjamin Walker, *The Hindu World*, 2 vols (New York: Praeger, 1968). There is much that is useful in S.N. Dasgupta, *History of Indian Philosophy* (5 vols, Cambridge University Press, 1922–55). Donald S. Lopez Jr (ed.), *Religions of India in Practice* (Princeton: Princeton University Press, 1995) is exceptional and unique.

Hindu religious literature is copious. Raimundo Panikkar's *The Vedic Experience* (Delhi: Motilal Banarsidass, 1994) provides a luminous introduction to the Vedas. The Upanishads are best experienced in the translations of Robert Hume (Oxford: Oxford University Press, 1983), S. Radhakrishnan (London: Allen and Unwin, 1953) and Swami Nikhilananda (London: Allen and Unwin, 1963). Of the hundreds of English translations of the *Bhagavad Gita*, those by Barbara S. Miller (London: Bantam, 1986), Stephen Mitchell (New York: Three Rivers Press, 2002) and Swami Prabhavananda and C. Isherwood (New York: New American Library, 1993) compel attention. See also *The Bhagavad Gita According to Gandhi* (Albany, CA: Berkeley Hills Books, 2000). There is no good contemporary English translation of the *Mahabharata* in its entirety, but the four volumes by J.A.B. van Buitenen (Chicago: University of Chicago Press, 1973) are superb, as are the five volumes (with two more in progress) of Valmiki's *Ramayana* by Robert Goldman and others (Princeton: Princeton University Press, 1984). The all-too-brief renderings of the *Mahabharata* (London: Viking, 1978) and *Ramayana* (London: Viking, 1980) by R.K. Narayan are nonetheless enlightening. P.V. Kane, *History of Dharmasastra* (5 vols, Poona: Bhandarkar Oriental Research Institute, 1930–62) remains the authoritative guide and is unlikely to be surpassed. Complete translations of many of the Mahapuranas are available in the *Ancient Indian Traditions and Mythology* Series, ed. J.L. Shastri (70 vols so far, Delhi: Motilal Banarsidass, 1970–). The Puranas can be sampled in Wendy O'Flaherty, *Hindu Myths* (London: Penguin, 1975).

The Bhakti poets have, for the most part, been poorly served by translators. But the following are superb works: A.K. Ramanujan, *Speaking of Siva* (London: Penguin, 1973); A.K. Ramanujan, *Hymns for the Drowning: Poems* for *Visnu by Nammalvar* (Princeton: Princeton University Press, 1981); E. Dimock and D. Levertov, *In Praise of Krishna* (New York: Anchor, 1967); *Jnaneshvari*, trans. V.G. Pradhan (London: Allen and Unwin, 1967); Kabir, *Bijak*, trans. Linda Hess (San Francisco: North Point Press, 1983); *Says Tuka*, trans. Dilip Chitre (London: Penguin, 1991); and Kenneth Bryant, *Poems to the Child-God* (Berkeley, CA: University of California Press, 1979).

Most of the godmen of contemporary India couldn't hold a candle to Sri Ramakrishna, most luminously encountered in *The Gospel of Sri Ramakrishna*, trans. Swami Nikhilananda (New York: Ramakrishna-Vivekananda Center, 1969), or Ramana Maharshi, *Talks with Sri Ramana Maharshi* (3 vols, Tiruvannamalai, n.d.). Christopher Isherwood, *Ramakrishna and His Disciples* (New York: Simon and Schuster, 1965) is mesmerizing. Nonetheless, among exponents of modern-day Hinduism, none is more important than Mohandas Gandhi: see his *Hindu Dharma* (Ahmedabad: Navajivan, 1950) and *What is Hinduism?* (Delhi: National Book Trust, 1994).

Other aspects of Hinduism receive remarkable treatment in Shashibhusan Dasgupta, *Obscure Religious Cults* (Calcutta: Firma KLM, 1969); Diana Eck, *Banaras: City of Light* (London: Routledge, 1983); Mircea Eliade, *Yoga: Immortality and Freedom* (Princeton: Princeton University Press, 1970); Stephen P. Huyler, *Meeting God: Elements of Hindu Devotion* (New Haven, CT: Yale University Press, 1999); and *The Complete Kama Sutra*, trans. Alain Danielou (Maine: Park Street Press, 1994). Gunther-Dietz Sontheimer and Herman Kulke provide a good introduction to the transformations within Hinduism in their compilation, *Hinduism Reconsidered* (Delhi: Manohar, 1997).

## Acknowledgements

The author would like to thank Ziauddin Sardar and Richard Appignanesi for entrusting him with this book, his friends in the Coalition for an Egalitarian and Pluralistic India – and in particular Shuklaji, Syeda, Robin, Monidipa, Tarun, Samee, Safoora, Mahdi [aka Mr Sufi], Asha, Shahed – for making Southern California less intolerable than he is otherwise inclined to find it, and Anju, Avni and Ishaan for enduring his at times manic working habits. This book is particularly for Professor I.K. Shukla, whose relentless commitment to Marxism and secularism have not interfered with his voluminous knowledge of Indian literary and religious traditions, and who has unstintingly given the benefit of his erudition to the author.

## About the Author

Vinay Lal teaches history and South Asian studies at the University of California, Los Angeles. His most recent books include *The History of History: Politics and Scholarship in Modern India* (Delhi: Oxford University Press, 2003); *Of Cricket, Guinness and Gandhi: Essays on Indian History and Culture* (Calcutta: Seagull Books, 2003); and *Empire of Knowledge: Culture and Plurality in the Global Economy* (London: Pluto, 2002).

## About the Illustrator

Borin Van Loon has created a total of fourteen "Introducing"-style books including Icon Books' *Introducing Darwin*, *Introducing Cultural Studies*, *Introducing Psychotherapy*, *Introducing Mathematics*, *Introducing Eastern Philosophy* and the best-selling *Introducing Buddha*. He is a surrealist painter and collagist who also produces the comic strip "A Severed Head" for *The Chap* magazine and has been a freelance illustrator since 1979. View his website on www.borinvanloon.co.uk

# Index